Primary Sources of World Cultures™

MEXICO

A PRIMARY SOURCE CULTURAL GUIDE

Allan B. Cobb

The Rosen Publishing Group's
PowerPlus Books™
New York

Published in 2004 by The Rosen Publishing Group, Inc.
29 East 21st Street, New York, NY 10010

Library of Congress Cataloging-in-Publication Data

Cobb, Allan B.
Mexico: a primary source cultural guide / by Allan B. Cobb.— 1st ed.
    p. cm. — (Primary sources of world cultures)
Summary: An overview of the history and culture of Mexico and its people including the geography, myths, arts, daily life, education, industry, and government, with illustrations from primary source documents.
Includes bibliographical references and index.
ISBN 0-8239-3840-9 (library binding)
1. Mexico—Juvenile literature. [1. Mexico.]
I. Title. II. Series.
F1208.5 .C63 2003
972—dc21

2002012128

Manufactured in the United States of America

Cover images: Colonial-style Santo Domingo Church in Oaxaca, Mexico *(left)*. A *charro*, or Mexican cowboy, in Guadalajara, Mexico *(right)*.

Photo Credits: Cover (background), pp. 42, 51, 62, 64 © Werner Forman Archive; cover (middle), cover (bottom), pp. 4 (bottom), 56, 76, 103 © Danny Lehman/Corbis; pp. 4 (top), 10, 15 © Robert Frerck/Woodfin Camp & Associates; pp. 4 (middle), 18, 20, 21 (bottom), 23, 30 (top), 70, 74, 81 (top) © Corbis; pp. 5 (top), 88 (top) © Carlos S. Pereyra/D. Donne Bryant Stock Photo; pp. 5 (middle), 93 © Bobbe Wolf/ImageState; pp. 5 (bottom), 30 (bottom), 34, 77, 81 (bottom), 82 (bottom), 87 (top), 110 © Matton; pp. 6, 48 © Stewart Aitchison/D. Donne Bryant Stock Photo; p. 7 © M. Borchi/Photo Researchers, Inc.; p. 8 © R. W. Gerling/D. Donne Bryant Stock Photo; p. 9 © Randy Faris/Corbis; p. 11 © Kal Miller/ Woodfin Camp & Associates; pp. 13, 33 (top), 72, 86 (bottom) © D. Donne Bryant Stock Photo; p. 16 © Lockwood/D. Donne Bryant Stock Photo; p. 17 © Stephanie Maze/Woodfin Camp & Associates; p. 19 © Edward Jones/Photo Researchers, Inc.; p. 21 (top), 40, 65 (top) © Bridgeman Art Library; p. 24 © Burstein Collection/Corbis; p. 25 © Dagli Orti/National History Museum, Mexico City/Art Archive; p. 26 © Giraudon/Art Resource; pp. 27, 32 (top) © Archivo Iconografico, S.A./Corbis; p. 28 © Photo Researchers, Inc.; p. 29 (top) © Hulton/Archive/Getty Images; p. 29 (bottom) © Center for American History, University of Texas, Austin, TX; pp. 31, 32 (bottom), 80 (top and bottom) © Bettmann/Corbis; p. 33 (bottom) © Jay W. Sharp/D. Donne Bryant Stock Photo; p. 35 © AFP/Corbis; pp. 36, 101 © Chris Sharp/Photo Researchers, Inc.; p. 37 © Mexican School/Codex Zouche Nuttall/Bridgeman Art Library; pp. 39, 102, 104 © Macduff Everton/Corbis; p. 41 © Sean Sprague/Bridgeman Art Library; p. 43 (top) © J. P. Courau/D. Donne Bryant Stock Photo; pp. 43 (bottom), 47 © Suzanne Murphy-Larronde/D. Donne Bryant Stock Photo; p. 45 © Robert Fried Photography; pp. 46, 95, 98, 105 © Jeff Greenberg/ImageState; p. 49 © Newberry Library; p. 50 © DUMA Acquisition Fund/Duke University Museum of Art; p. 52 © Eric and David Hosking/Corbis; pp. 53, 59 (bottom), 113 (top) © Reuters NewMedia Inc./Corbis; p. 54 © Clasos Agencia International/Corbis Sygma; p. 57 © Jan Butchofsky-Houser/Corbis; p. 59 (top) © Catherine Karnow/Corbis; p. 60 © Viesti & Associates; p. 61 © Keith Dannemiller/Corbis SABA; p. 63 © British Museum, London/Bridgeman Art Library; pp. 65 (bottom), 73 © SEF/Art Resource; p. 66 (top) © The Granger Collection; p. 66 (bottom) © Zabe/AMI/Art Resource; p. 67 © Ivan Orta/D. Donne Bryant Stock Photo; p. 68 © Gilles Mermet/AKG London; p. 69 © Biblioteca Nacional, Madrid/Bridgeman Art Library; p. 71 © H. Huntly Hersch/D. Donne Bryant Stock Photo; p. 75 © Dagli Orti/National Anthropological Museum, Mexico/Art Archive; p. 79 © Schalkwijk/2003 Banco de Mexico Diego Rivera & Frida Kahlo Museums Trust/Art Resource; p. 82 (top) © Alison Wright/Photo Researchers, Inc.; p. 83 © Lindsay Hebberd/Corbis; p. 84 © John Bigelow Taylor/Art Resource; p. 85 © Werner Forman/Art Resource; p. 86 (top) © Art Resource; pp. 87 (bottom), 114 © AFP; p. 88 (bottom) © Wesley Bocxe/Photo Researchers, Inc.; pp. 89, 90, 94 © George Ancona/ImageState; p. 91 © Patricia Teja Roell/ImageState; p. 92 © Richard A. Cooke/Corbis; p. 97 © Andre Jenny/ImageState; p. 99 © Craig Roney/D. Donne Bryant Stock Photo; p. 100 © Robert Fried/D. Donne Bryant Stock Photo; p. 106 © Tim Mantoani/ImageState; p. 108 © Hollenbeck Photography ImageState; p. 109 © Cliff Hollenbeck/ImageState; p. 111 © Carlos S. Pereyra/D. Donne Bryant Stock Photo; p. 112 © Jean-Gerard Sidaner/Photo Researchers, Inc.; p. 113 (bottom) © Cindy Reiman; p. 121 © Superstock.

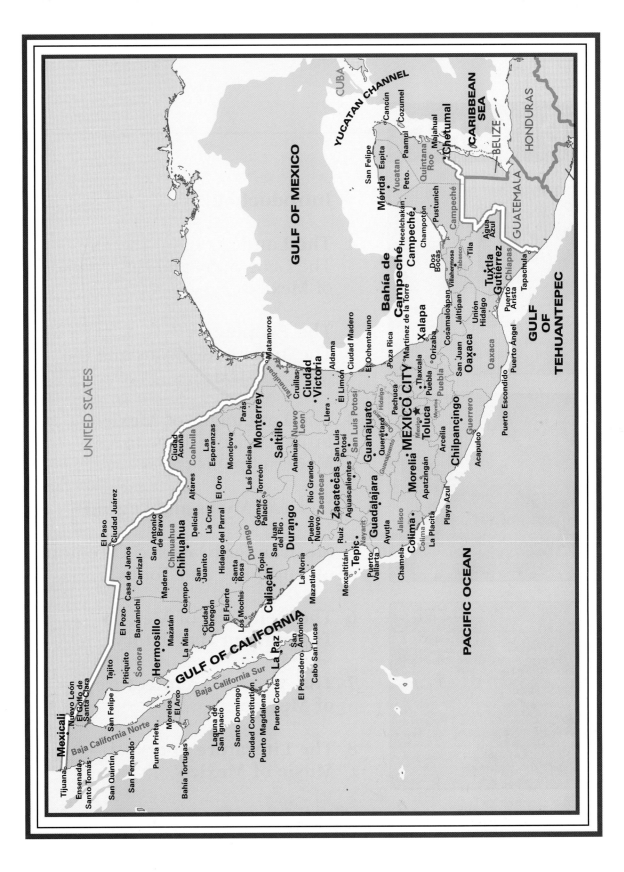

CONTENTS

INTRODUCTION

Mexico is a country that traces its cultural roots back more than thirty centuries. Ranging from beaches to rain forests, from deserts to snowcapped mountains, Mexico is a land where many civilizations rose and fell long before the Spanish arrived in the sixteenth century. Under Spanish rule, Mexico was transformed into a colony with a government based on a mixture of European ideas and local customs.

While many native peoples converted to Catholicism at the urging of the Spanish, the people of Mexico have retained parts of their ancient heritage, shaping their lifestyle into a colorful blend of European and Indian traditions. Most people in Mexico speak Spanish, although a large number still speak one of the ancient Indian languages. Mexican people have a love of festivals and ceremonies. Traditional food, clothing, and music play important parts in their observances and celebrations. Mexicans, who eat an incredible variety of foods, introduced the world to many important vegetables, such as corn, potatoes, and tomatoes. Present-day Mexican cuisine continues to be influenced by its ancient and European roots.

Mexico's eventful past has strongly influenced its art and architecture. Modern buildings are built on top of or next to buildings that are hundreds or even thousands of years old.

Mexico has been an important force in the literary world of Latin America. And, as technology becomes more widespread, Mexico prepares to play a bigger role in the world economy. All of these factors combine to create a unique and fascinating country.

At twenty-two miles long, Bahia Concepcion *(left)* is the largest bay on the Sea of Cortez. Several small islands that dot the coastline are excellent for fishing, snorkeling, and sunbathing. The Ball Court *(above)* in the Puuc Region is where the sacred Mayan ball games took place. Two teams fought against each other to pass a solid rubber ball through a ring, which represented the portal to the otherworld. The Maya played this game to reenact the moment when the third creation of the world ended and the fourth began.

THE LAND

1

The Geography and Environment of Mexico

Mexico is located on the continent of North America. Because it sits at the bottom of North America, just above South America, it is sometimes called Middle America. It has a total land area of 761,600 square miles (1,972,550 square kilometers), which is slightly less than three times the size of Texas. Mexico is the third largest country in Latin America, behind Brazil and Argentina. Latin American countries are those in which people speak Spanish or Portuguese.

To the north, Mexico borders the United States. Its southern border meets Guatemala and Belize. Mexico shares 1,952 miles (3,141 km) of border with the United States, 598 miles (962 km) of border with Guatemala, and 155 miles (250 km) with Belize. Mexico's coastline extends for 5,798 miles (9,330 km) along the Pacific Ocean, the Gulf of Mexico, and the Caribbean Sea.

Political Divisions

The official name of Mexico is Los Estados Unidos Mexicanos (the United States of Mexico). Mexico is divided into thirty-one *estados* (states) and the *Distrito Federal* (federal district).

The Mountains

Two mountain chains run through Mexico; they are the northern extension of the Andes mountains, which begin in South America. When the range reaches

The Sierra Madre Occidental mountain range *(left)* in Mexico runs parallel to the Gulf of Mexico and the Pacific Ocean. With an average elevation of 10,000 feet, many of the mountains are volcanic and a few have snowcapped peaks. Mexican farmers cultivate fields of agave *(above)* for the production of tequila. When the Spaniards conquered Mexico in the 1500s, they brought their knowledge of distillation and used native ingredients to create beverages to suit their tastes.

Barranca del Cobre, the Copper Canyon, derives its name from the copper green lichen present on the canyon walls. This canyon system is four times larger than the Grand Canyon.

Mexico, it splits in two. The Sierra Madre Occidental range, the western chain, links up with the Rocky Mountains in the United States and continues into Canada. The Sierra Madre Oriental range, the eastern chain, extends into Texas.

The Sierra Madre Occidental range contains some of Mexico's most rugged land. It was a natural barrier to travel between central Mexico and the Pacific coast until the 1900s, when paved roads and rail lines were built across the mountains.

Short, steep mountain streams running through this range cut deep canyons on their way to the Pacific Ocean. Some of the canyons are 8,280 feet (1.6 km) deep. La Barranca del Cobre (Copper Canyon), the largest and most well known, is so wide, deep, and remote that parts of the canyon remain unexplored.

The Sierra Madre Oriental range is less rugged than the Sierra Madre Occidental. It is more like a series of mountain ranges with passes around them. For hundreds of years, people have been building roads through the mountains. Train tracks were laid there in the 1800s. Some areas contain considerable deposits of iron ore, coal, silver, and fluorite. Spaniards began mining for these minerals in the 1500s; in many places, mining continues to this day.

The Land

Mexico is divided into six main land regions—the Pacific Northwest, the Plateau of Mexico, the Gulf Coastal Plain, the Southern Uplands, the Chiapas Highlands,

and the Yucatán Peninsula. These regions are further divided into smaller areas based on their elevation, climate, and land formations.

The peninsula of Baja California, Mexico, ranges from desert to semitropical to mountainous regions. It also contains pine forests and beaches.

Pacific Northwest

The Pacific Northwest is a dry region. It includes the peninsula of Baja California as well as mountains and desert. The Pacific Northwest is considered the southern end of the huge Imperial Valley in California. The lowest point in elevation, near Mexicali, is 33 feet (10 meters) below sea level. This area contains many important mineral resources such as copper, silver, manganese, and fluorite.

The Pacific Northwest also has some of the most fertile soil in Mexico. Because much of the area is desert, agriculture is only possible in a few places near the coast where there is enough rainfall to grow crops. The fertile zone is a narrow strip that follows the coast on the mainland. Here, waters from the Colorado, Fuerte, Yaqui, and other rivers provide irrigation for farmland. Cotton and wheat are the two most important crops. Cattle are also raised here.

Plateau of Mexico

Most of Mexico's people live in the Plateau of Mexico, the largest region in the country. With a wide variety of landforms, the Plateau of Mexico lies between two mountain ranges, the Sierra Madre Occidental on the west and the Sierra Madre Oriental on the east.

The Cordillera Neo-Volcánica is a series of volcanoes on the plateau's southern edge. Pico de Orizaba is the highest peak in Mexico at 18,410 feet (5,610 m). Popocatépetl and Iztaccíhuatl, two volcanoes that tower over Mexico City, are more than 17,000 feet (5,180 m) high. The rich, fertile soil and ample rain allow crops, including corn and beans, to grow. In fact, these areas have been used as farmland for at least 10,000 years. Nearby is Lake Chapala. Covering 417 square miles (1,080 square km), it is the largest lake in Mexico.

The central part of the Plateau of Mexico is the Mesa Central (Central Plateau), with an average elevation of about 7,000 feet (2,100 m). The rich soil and plentiful rainfall create an agricultural paradise for growing corn, beans, wheat, and barley.

Mexico City, the capital of Mexico, is located within the plateau. The city was built on the site of the Aztec capital, Tenochtitlán.

The Mesa del Norte (Northern Plateau) extends from the Mesa Central to the United States border. Elevations in this large area range from about 4,000 feet to 9,000 feet (about 1,200 m to 2,700 m). Because the Mesa del Norte is fairly dry, agriculture is limited to areas where there is water for irrigation. The higher the elevation, the colder the climate, making frequent frost a constant threat to crops.

Gulf Coastal Plain

The Gulf Coastal Plain is located on the eastern side of the country, along the Gulf of Mexico. North of Tampico, the dry coastal plain is predominantly covered with low thorny bushes, cacti, and small trees. Agriculture is clustered around rivers that provide water for irrigation. Corn, cotton, oranges, and sorghum (for cattle feed) are common crops. South of Tampico, where the coastal plain receives more rainfall, low bushes and trees give way to lush tropical vegetation. Some areas have rich soil suitable for growing bananas, sugarcane, corn, and rice.

The central Chiapas Highlands are eight thousand feet above the Grijalva River. For at least a thousand years, they have been home to the Tzotzil- and Tzeltal-speaking Maya who live near limestone springs fed by underground rivers.

Southern Uplands

The Southern Uplands are located just south of the Plateau of Mexico. The Sierra Madre del Sur mountains run along the Pacific Coast. Famous beach resorts such as Puerto Escondido and Acapulco are located along the coast in this region. The Oaxaca Plateau, on the eastern part of the Southern Uplands, was a major political center in ancient times. This region has many mineral resources such as gold, silver, mercury, and jade.

Chiapas Highlands

Close to the border with Guatemala, the Chiapas Highlands, a block-like mountainous area, rises more than 9,000 feet (2,700 m) above sea level. The region contains many tablelands, broad flat areas at high elevations. Coffee, fruit, corn, and beans are grown in the broad river valleys and on ancient agricultural terraces. This area is home to many people who, descended from ancient peoples, still speak Maya and other languages that are more than 2,000 years old.

Yucatán Peninsula

The Yucatán Peninsula is best known for its tropical vacation spots. Cancún and Cozumel are two popular travel destinations, where vacationers enjoy beaches and turquoise waters.

Most of the Yucatán Peninsula is fairly dry. In the north, the vegetation is mostly small bushes and trees. Toward the south, the peninsula becomes wetter and the vegetation becomes more like that of a tropical jungle. Because of the geology of the area, the soil is usually thin. As a result, there is little farming, although a small amount of corn is grown.

The Yucatán Peninsula is a low limestone plateau. Lacking rivers, water comes from a vast system of caves, many lying below the land's surface. Sometimes the limestone surface collapses into a cave, causing an opening. Called cenotes, the openings are usually straight-walled caverns leading down to the water, like a well. Cenotes were as important a source of water for the ancient Maya as they are for today's farmers. Cenotes were also used by the Maya as sacred ceremonial sites.

Climate

The climate of Mexico varies greatly from region to region and sometimes even within a region. In the tropical regions of Mexico, a lot of rain usually falls in the summer months. This is called the rainy season. During this period, thunderclouds

Cancún, a sixteen-mile-long island with one road and a population of about 400,000 people, is a popular tourist spot. With an average temperature of 80°F, it enjoys 280 days of sunshine a year.

gather during the day, and short, heavy showers drop rain in the afternoon. Farther south into the tropics, the rainy season usually starts earlier and lasts longer. During the rest of the year, called the dry season, rains are usually more moderate.

Most of northern Mexico is desert or semidesert. Rain does not fall in predictable seasons as it does in the tropics. However, most of the rainfall occurs in the summer months during afternoon thunderstorms. Usually, these showers do not take place daily, as in the tropics. The lack of rain has always limited Mexico's agriculture to areas that have water available for irrigation.

In most of the desert areas, the days are hot in the summer with cool nights. In winter, days are warm and nights are cold.

Temperatures usually do not vary as much in the tropical areas of Mexico. Elevation is what controls climate the most in these places. In regions below 3,000 feet (900 m), the climate is called *tierra caliente* (hot land). The summers are long and hot, and the winters are mild with temperatures rarely below freezing. Between 3,000 and 6,000 feet (900 and 1,800 m), the area is called the *tierra templada* (temperate land). The summer and winter temperatures are more moderate, usually between 50°F and 80°F (10°C and 27°C). Above 6,000 feet (1,800 m), the area is called the *tierra fria* (cold land). Frost is rare, but the temperatures are often cooler than in the tierra templada. Some of the highest mountain peaks are always covered with snow.

Plants and Animals

About 26 percent of Mexico is forest or woodlands. Depending on the area, these forests have valuable hardwoods such as oak, mahogany, rosewood, and walnut. Mexico also has large forests of pines in the mountains that are used for lumber and as pulp for the paper industry. In some areas of Mexico, harvesting timber is important to the local economy.

Mexico also has a wide variety of cacti. These range from tiny ones to the giant organ-pipe cactus. Mexico also has many kinds of flowers and grasses. In the tropical rain forests, hundreds of species of orchids and bromeliads add color to the forest. Pineapples are the fruit of bromeliads.

In northern Mexico, deer, coyotes, black bears, mountain lions, raccoons, bats, skunks, prairie dogs, and rattlesnakes are common. Monkeys, jaguars, ocelots, alligators, and tapirs live in the tropical areas.

Mexico is filled with birds, ranging from tiny hummingbirds to majestic golden eagles to colorful parrots and macaws. Mexico is an important wintering ground for many migratory birds.

Many kinds of fish live in Mexico's rivers and lakes. Popular sport fish are bass, catfish, and trout. In the oceans, game fish such as red snapper, redfish, marlin, and swordfish are valuable resources. Many varieties of brightly colored tropical fish live in the coral reefs along the Caribbean coast.

Natural Resources

Mexico's natural resources are important to its economy. Timber is found in both the mountains of northern Mexico and the rain forests of southern Mexico. Petroleum and natural gas are plentiful along the Gulf Coast plain and offshore in the Gulf of Mexico and the Bay of Campeche. The mountains in Mexico yield many minerals, including silver, copper, gold, lead, zinc, and fluorite.

Baird's tapirs thrive in the swampy jungles or river habitats of Mexico, Central America, and Colombia. These creatures are herbivores, feeding mainly on green shoots and leaves of plants that grow in water. With a keen sense of hearing and smell, they communicate by making shrill whistling sounds.

An aerial view of Mexico City shows the severity of its atmospheric pollution, caused mostly by vehicle exhaust. Mexico City is located in a basin 7,400 feet above sea level, where the surrounding mountains block the city from winds. As a result, warm air sits above a surface layer of cold air, trapping poisonous emissions below.

Land Use

Land is precious in Mexico. The amount available for growing crops is only about 12 percent of the country. Only 1 percent of the land is used to grow fruit and nuts. Permanent pasture for grazing cattle, horses, goats, and sheep makes up another 39 percent. Forests and woodlands cover 26 percent of the country. The remaining 22 percent is too mountainous or too urban for agriculture.

Environmental Issues

Vast portions of Mexico have too little rainfall, making it difficult to find clean water. In addition, many urban areas suffer with improperly treated sewage, polluted storm water runoff, and industrial waste.

Deforestation is another environmental problem facing Mexico. Poor logging practices and poor land management contribute to the loss of valuable topsoil, which chokes life out of Mexico's rivers and lakes. Some areas of Mexico suffer from desertification, a condition in which the edges of land turn to desert. While a natural process, poor land management and poor farming methods speed up the loss of useful soil.

The large urban areas suffer from the worst air pollution in the world, mostly from cars. Mexico has not had strict clean air regulations. The government now works toward solving the problem, but it will be a long time before the World Health Organization finds the air at an acceptably safe level.

tenochtitlan

col huacan. pueblo.   te nayucan. 2pueblo/

THE PEOPLE

2

The Ancient Mexicans and the Modern Mexicans

Mexico is considered the cradle of civilization in North and South America. The period before Christopher Columbus arrived in the New World (in 1492) is referred to as the pre-Columbian era. During this time, Mexico was one of the first places in the New World where ancient peoples settled, changing their lifestyle from that of nomadic hunters and gatherers to farmers who grew crops. Corn, one of the earliest harvested plants in the Western Hemisphere, helped to shape the history of Mexico for more than 10,000 years. It remains an important force in the country.

Pre-Columbian Times

Many historians believe that the earliest people came to the Americas from Siberia 30,000 to 40,000 years ago. They traveled across land or an ice bridge over the Bering Strait. This bridge, which no longer exists, connected Siberia (Russia) to Alaska during the Ice Age. Arriving in small groups, people were either escaping from danger or following animal herds. People spread out across North America and began moving south, eventually reaching the tip of South America.

These early arrivals are called Paleolithic or Stone Age people because they made their tools out of stones or rocks. They hunted deer, wild horses, and small animals using traps, slings, and spears. They also used atlatls (tools to throw spears harder and farther) to hunt large game such as mammoths, camels, bison, and bears. Archaeologists have found artifacts made from stone and bone as well as remains of campfires that are 20,000 years old.

An Aztec illumination *(left)* shows the founding of Tenochtitlán, which was built in 1325 on an island in Lake Texcoco. The Angel of Independence statue *(above)* in Mexico City commemorates Mexico's struggle for independence from Spain between 1810 and 1821. Italian artist Enrique Alciati won the competition for the best design. The statue was unveiled on September 16, 1910. It was a gift from France.

Cave paintings at the archaeological site Cueva Pintada in Baja California, cover 500 feet of wall space, mostly with images of wildlife. Beyond recognizing that they were completed by indigenous people between 100 BC and AD 1300, archaeologists know little else about them.

Near Mexico City, mammoth bones have been found that have spear points embedded in them. Little is known about the lives of the early people in Mexico. Few fossilized human bones have been found. As these Stone Age peoples were nomadic, traveling across Mexico in small groups to follow animal herds, they left behind very little evidence of their lives.

By about 8000 BC, many tribes or clans of ancient peoples roamed through the Plateau of Mexico. Hunters and gatherers, they followed herds of buffalo, mammoths, and mastodons. They also gathered a wide variety of edible plants as they hunted. Food was plentiful, as the climate was much wetter than today. The area was rich with plants, animals, and clean water.

By about 7500 BC, the climate became arid, or dry. The large mammals such as bison, mammoths, and camels began to disappear in Mexico and all over North America. To survive, the native peoples had to rely on smaller animals and edible plants.

As plants became more important in their diet, people began to change their lifestyle. With herds of large animals gone, the native people (also referred to today as Indians) no longer needed to follow game. Instead, they settled near places where edible plants grew and water was available. The Indians learned to grow plants for food, bringing agriculture to Mexico.

The People: The Ancient Mexicans and the Modern Mexicans

An illustration from a Maya codex, circa 900, depicts a priest sowing corn at an annual ceremony. The cultivation of corn in Mexico can be traced back 7,000 years.

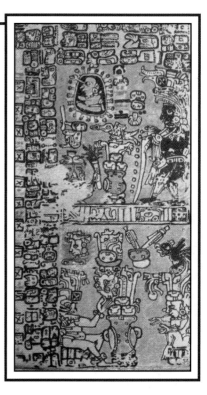

One of the places Indians first settled was in the central valley of Mexico, near Tehuacán in the modern state of Puebla. This area had a good climate, abundant water, and good soil for growing crops. The Indians raised avocados, beans, peppers, squashes, and tomatoes. They also began to grow a type of grass with edible seeds. Through selective breeding, the Indians created a plant that grew seeds that were larger and more nutritious. This new plant is what we know as corn. Corn quickly became the staple crop because it was easy to grow and had a high crop yield.

Because corn grew so plentifully, it was easy to grow more than a family needed in a year. Having extra corn meant villages could feed more and more people. Populations increased, and within the larger villages, people were freed from working in fields or hunting, so they could develop other skills. For example, some people began to make pottery, others wove cloth, and others traded for goods with people from different regions.

Religions developed, with people worshiping gods that represented natural forces such as rain, the sun, and the moon. As religion began to play a more important role in people's lives, the Indians began to build more and more elaborate temples for worship. Some villages became religious centers, with large temples in the shape of tall flat-topped pyramids.

The Olmec culture flourished between 1200 and 400 BC. Because no written records of the Olmec civilization survive, information is gathered through archaeological exploration, which uncovers architecture, ceramics, tools, and sculpture. This statue of an Olmec priest holds an infant thought to have supernatural powers.

The first great civilization of Mexico developed along the southern Gulf Coast. The Indians who started this early civilization are known as the Olmecs. Their civilization flourished between about 1200 BC and 400 BC. The Olmecs, who are probably best known for their carved stone heads and other sculptures, which weigh up to several tons, developed a complex calendar and a counting system. Their accomplishments led the way for many other great civilizations in Mexico and throughout Central America and South America.

The Classic Period

After the decline of the Olmec civilization, three civilizations sprang up in different parts of Mexico. Begun around AD 250, this era lasted to around AD 900. Known for its art and architecture, this is called Mexico's classic period.

The first of these three civilizations developed just north of present-day Mexico City. Little is known of these people, who we call the Teotihuacanos, but their capital city, called Teotihuacán, was one of the greatest cities in the world at its time. Today, Teotihuacán is one of the most visited archaeological sites in Mexico. By AD 700, about 125,000 people lived in the city. The people of Teotihuacán built huge pyramids dedicated to the sun and the moon. The art, architecture, and culture of this city influenced many other civilizations throughout North, South, and Central America. Around AD 800, the civilization collapsed and the people abandoned the city.

The Zapotec Indians emerged as a civilization in what is now Oaxaca. The Zapotecs flattened an entire mountaintop to build their capital city, Monte Albán. Constructing their buildings of huge stone blocks, the Zapotec people built tall temples as well as elaborate palaces and houses. Because the climate in the region is so dry, many of these structures are still well preserved today. The Zapotec civilization collapsed around AD 800.

The Mayan civilization flourished around the same time. The Maya built cities throughout southern Mexico and the Yucatán Peninsula as well as in Belize, Guatemala, El Salvador, and Honduras. The Maya are the best known of all the ancient civilizations of Mexico. In addition to building great pyramids, huge palaces, and elaborate homes, the Maya developed a written language and recorded much of

Spanish conquistador Hernán Cortés designed this map of Tenochtitlán. Although a natural barrier of water surrounds the island, Cortés was able to enter the Aztec city in 1519 and conquer it in 1521. After Cortés's victory, the king named Cortés governor and captain general of New Spain.

their history on stone monuments and on bark tablets. Their written language is still being deciphered today. The Maya also developed advanced mathematical skills and performed complex calculations on the movements of the sun, the moon, and the planets. The Maya were the first people to develop the concept of zero.

The Mayan calendar, which accounted for all 365 days of the year, was much more advanced than the Olmec calendar. The Maya also made colorful pottery and intricately woven textiles. The Mayan civilization, like the others at the time, collapsed around AD 900.

No one knows why these great civilizations fell apart around the same time, but there are many theories. One idea suggests that prolonged droughts or crop diseases affected the corn. Another theory suggests that a change in the nature of warfare led to the collapses. Yet another suggestion is that the lower classes revolted against the upper classes. Archaeologists continue to study the remains of these civilizations to discover what happened. When the civilizations collapsed, the people moved out of their great cities and returned to a simpler rural life

The ancient Mayan city of Campeche is a World Heritage site. The World Heritage Committee helps make sure it survives for future generations. This classic period Campeche tripod plate, dated between 500 and 800, shows a figure holding a heart-shaped plant.

The Toltecs and Aztecs

After the fall of the civilizations of the classic period, the Toltecs controlled many parts of Mexico. They took over many of the Mayan sites in the Yucatán. Ruling from their capital at Tula, located north of present-day Mexico City, they used force to maintain their empire. The Toltecs were defeated around AD 1200 by the Chichimec people. But the Chichimecs lacked the political and economic skills to maintain a large empire, and it fell apart.

The Aztecs were the last of the great ancient civilizations in Mexico. The Aztec empire started in the mid-1400s; it rapidly expanded to include much of Central Mexico, as the Aztecs conquered many Indian tribes throughout the region. Fierce

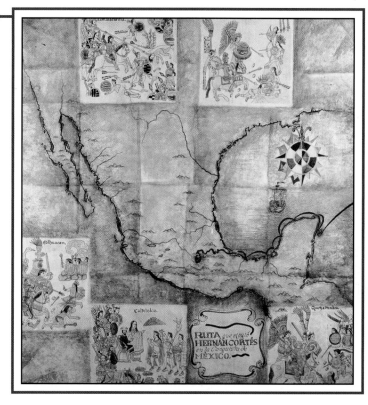

A map illustrates the route taken by Hernán Cortés during his conquest of Mexico. Cortés followed the coastline and founded Veracruz, the first Spanish settlement in Mexico. Here he appointed a town council and gave himself the title of captain general, with authority under Spanish law to conquer Mexico.

warriors, the Aztecs captured many prisoners during wars, enslaving or sacrificing their captives. The Aztecs, who demanded taxes from the people they conquered, amassed great wealth in gold, silver, and other treasures. From their capital at Tenochtitlán, the Aztecs controlled their empire through terror. During the dedication of one of their temples, it is believed they sacrificed 20,000 people in a single day. Even though the Aztecs were ruthless, Tenochtitlán became a center for arts, pottery, music, poetry, and medicine. By 1491, Tenochtitlán had a population of about 300,000 people.

The Spanish

With Christopher Columbus's arrival in the New World, the Spanish began to occupy the West Indies. The Spanish explored the Caribbean, and in 1517 a Spanish expedition reached Mexico. Francisco Fernández de Córdoba sailed to the Yucatán Peninsula and learned about the great cities that existed there. In 1518, a second expedition, led by Juan de Grijalva, explored the coast of Mexico from the Yucatán Peninsula to modern-day Veracruz. News of the foreign explorers reached Tenochtitlán and the emperor Montezuma II. The Aztecs had never seen anything like the Spaniards—they rode horses, they wore armor, and they had guns and cannons.

In 1519, a third Spanish expedition, led by Hernán Cortés, was sent to Mexico. Cortés sailed with 650 men and 22 ships. Cortés and his soldiers, called conquistadors, were a well-equipped and ruthless army. In addition to having guns and cannons, they wore protective armor. Landing on the Mexican coast, the Spanish established the city of Veracruz. The Spaniards easily defeated the local Indians. To escape being killed, many of the tribes became allies with the Spanish. When Montezuma II heard of the battles, he sent treasures to Cortés; Montezuma thought Cortés was a god. Montezuma II also asked him to leave his country.

Instead of leaving, Cortés set out with his army to conquer the Aztecs and their capital, Tenochtitlán. He expected to find more treasures. Cortés and his conquistadors were joined by thousands of Indian allies. These Indians considered the Aztecs their enemy; they hoped to defeat the Aztecs with the help of the Spanish and regain their freedom.

When the Spaniards first arrived at Tenochtitlán, the Aztecs were welcoming. This changed when Cortés captured Montezuma II and held him hostage. Cortés and the conquistadors demanded a ransom from the Aztec people in the form of gold and silver.

After about six months, the Aztecs revolted. The Spaniards and Aztecs fought bloody battles for about a week before the Spaniards tried to escape from Tenochtitlán. When they were discovered, hundreds of Spaniards were killed in a battle known as *la noche triste* (the sad night). Cortés and many of his men barely

A fresco painting by Miguel Gonzalez dating from 1519 shows Montezuma II kneeling before Hernán Cortés at the Spanish conquistadors' victory over the Aztecs. Cortés conquered the Aztec Empire of 5 million people with an army of less than 600 men, supported by 20 horses and 10 cannons.

escaped. Six months later, Cortés returned to Tenochtitlán with more conquistadors, surrounded the city, cut off food and water supplies, and eventually captured the city. Once Tenochtitlán was captured, Montezuma II was killed and the Spanish took over most of the Aztec Empire.

The Spanish also brought a variety of diseases to Mexico, including cholera and smallpox. The Indians of Mexico had no resistance to these germs. Epidemics swept across Mexico. War and disease took their toll on the native population. Within twenty years of the arrival of the Spanish, an estimated 19 million Indians—95 percent of the population—had died.

The Spanish established programs to convert the Indians to Catholicism. The Catholic Church began building missions and churches throughout Mexico. The Spanish also began to mine in the rich mineral regions using the Indians as slaves. For more than 100 years, the Spanish worked to transform the New World into their image of an ideal colony. The Spanish grew rich using the Indians as slaves. The Indians, however, were growing tired of this treatment.

On September 15, 1810, a priest named Miguel Hidalgo y Costilla gave a late-night speech. His speech, *El Grito de Dolores* (The cry of Dolores), called for rebellion against the Spanish government so that Mexicans could govern themselves. The uprising that began that day lasted for six years before the Spaniards crushed it.

Independence

In 1820, problems in Spain weakened the power of King Ferdinand VII, and another revolt began in Mexico. Agustín de Iturbide was given command of the Spanish army in Mexico and was ordered to stop the rebellion. Instead of fighting, he met with Vicente Guerrero and they worked together to

This statue of Benito Juárez, national hero and past president of Mexico, overlooks his hometown of Oaxaca. Juárez is regarded as the greatest hero in Mexico's history as a result of his progressive reforms.

The first president of Mexico, Guadalupe Victoria (1786–1872), studied at the seminary in Durango but was prompted by Miguel Hidalgo to join the independence struggle. Victoria's administration had a strong foreign policy, receiving recognition of Mexico's independence from European powers. However, Victoria did little to improve the domestic economy of Mexico.

achieve Mexican independence from Spain. The Spanish army in Mexico and the rebel forces joined together to drive out those loyal to Spain. By the end of 1821, Mexico was an independent nation.

Setting up the new government was difficult, but after three years of argument and compromise, it took shape. Mexico became a republic with a president, a two-house congress to run the country, and governors and legislatures to run each state. The first president of Mexico was Guadalupe Victoria.

War with Texas and the United States

The new government of Mexico had problems because many Mexicans did not support the constitution. There was so much political fighting between the factions that it was difficult to get anything accomplished.

Mexico sent troops to Texas under the command of General Antonio López de Santa Anna. After many bloody battles in Texas, Santa Anna's army was defeated

The Alamo in San Antonio was under siege while delegates prepared the Texas Declaration of Independence. This document, signed on March 2, 1836, declared Texas a free and independent republic.

The Treaty of Guadalupe Hidalgo, signed on February 2, 1848, ended the war between Mexico and the United States. As a result, the United States gained 1,193,061 square miles of land.

at the Battle of San Jacinto. Texas gained its independence from Mexico and later joined the United States.

Military forces from the United States occupied territories claimed by Mexico in areas that are now New Mexico, Arizona, and California. In 1847, Santa Anna fought against U.S. troops at the Battle of Buena Vista near Saltillo, Mexico, and both sides claimed victory. The U.S. troops moved on and captured Mexico City in 1847. In 1848, the Treaty of Guadalupe Hidalgo was signed and the Mexican-American War ended.

The United States took possession of present-day California, Nevada, Utah, Colorado, and part of Arizona and New Mexico. The border of Texas was established at the Rio Grande river. In exchange for the territory, Mexico received $15 million. The Gadsden Purchase was made in 1853, and Mexico received $10 million for the remainder of Arizona and New Mexico, which established the present border between the United States and Mexico.

Reform

After the war with the United States, the government of Mexico was weak and almost broke. Santa Anna seized the government and installed himself as dictator. He remained in power until 1855, when he was removed from office.

A 1916 cartoon by Clifford Berryman titled "Carranza and Uncle Sam" depicts the United States and Mexico discussing how to divide lands during the reorganization of Mexico.

In 1855 elections were held for a new president. The winner was a Zapotec Indian named Benito Juárez. He and his followers supported private ownership of land, and they passed laws that took land from the Catholic Church and turned it over to Indian villages. Benito Juárez became a hero of the people. He is still revered as the common Indian who became president of Mexico.

Civil war broke out in 1855 between supporters of Juárez and the Catholic Church. This was called the War of the Reform. Juárez and his supporters prevailed. They passed laws that created a separation between church and state, taking much more land from the Catholic Church and weakening its power.

This lithograph of Benito Juárez, created during his presidency, was accompanied by a caption that stated, "He was of Native American ancestry and worked to transfer power from Mexicans of Spanish descent to all Mexicans."

Porfirio Díaz

Porfirio Díaz, a general in the Mexican army, overthrew Juárez's successor, Sebastián Lerdo de Tejada, in a military coup in 1876. Díaz served as president of Mexico from 1876 to 1882 and 1886 to 1911. Díaz used his control of the army to act as a dictator and intimidate his opponents. This harsh period of Mexican history is called Porfiriato. Even though Díaz and his

The French Invade Mexico!

In 1862, French forces invaded Mexico, capturing Mexico City. Benito Juárez fled, and Maximilian of France was named emperor of Mexico. Juárez and his supporters fought against the French but had little success.

In 1866, the United States demanded that the French remove their troops from Mexico. The French did not want to enter into a dispute with the United States, so they withdrew. Juárez returned to Mexico City and took over as president, remaining in office until his death in 1872.

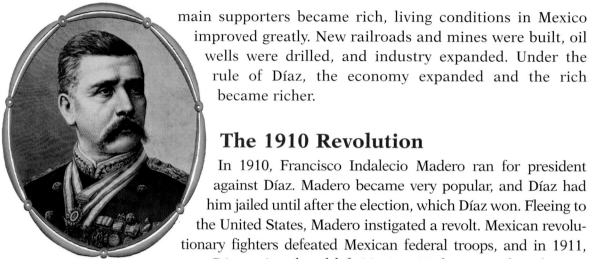

main supporters became rich, living conditions in Mexico improved greatly. New railroads and mines were built, oil wells were drilled, and industry expanded. Under the rule of Díaz, the economy expanded and the rich became richer.

The 1910 Revolution

In 1910, Francisco Indalecio Madero ran for president against Díaz. Madero became very popular, and Díaz had him jailed until after the election, which Díaz won. Fleeing to the United States, Madero instigated a revolt. Mexican revolutionary fighters defeated Mexican federal troops, and in 1911, Díaz resigned and left Mexico. Madero was elected president, but he was unable to control the factions or run the country. He was murdered in 1913. General Victoriano Huerta assumed power as a dictator. Venustiano Carranza started another revolution and took control.

Porfirio Díaz, shown in this 1884 portrait, was a Mixtec Indian with traces of Spanish blood. As a result of his harsh dictatorial rule, Díaz was forced to flee the country in 1911. He died in exile.

The Constitution of 1917

The leaders of the revolution struggled. Carranza remained in control as his troops fought against the rebel troops of Francisco "Pancho" Villa and Emiliano Zapata. The United States supported Carranza, helping him fight his enemies. By 1917, Carranza defeated his opponents. A newly written constitution gave the government control over agricultural properties, oil properties, the educational system, and the Roman

Revolutionary leader Francisco Madero and his men *(left)* in the late 1800s. After a revolution in April 1910, Madero replaced Porfirio Díaz as president. Emiliano Zapata *(top left, page 33)* was a Mexican revolutionary who fought in guerrilla actions during and after the Mexican Revolution. His goal was to seize all foreign-owned land and all land taken from villages. Pancho Villa, a Mexican rebel leader, is pictured at lower right *(page 33)*.

General Carranza works at his desk in Durango. The Mexican Revolution, which lasted from 1910 to 1917, ended with General Carranza becoming president. He created Mexico's current constitution.

Catholic Church. The president of Mexico was limited to one term, and laborers were allowed to form unions to protect their rights.

In the 1920s and 1930s, details of the new government continued to be worked out. The Roman Catholic Church was allowed to operate without government interference. Workers' rights improved and so did wages. New political parties formed, and people were allowed to vote freely in elections. The days of bloody revolutions and dictators were over.

The Current Government

Today the government of Mexico is a federal republic. It is based on the United States's constitutional theory and civil law system. A variety of political parties exist. The three most popular are the Institutional Revolutionary Party (PRI), the National Action Party (PAN), and the Party of the Democratic Revolution (PRD).

In December 2000, Congress greeted Mexican president Vicente Fox after he received the presidential sash. Fox's presidency put an end to more than seven decades of unbroken leadership by the Institutional Revolutionary Party (PRI).

In 2000, Vicente Fox Quesada was elected president of Mexico. The president, whose term lasts six years, appoints a cabinet to run the subdivisions of the executive branch.

The legislative branch contains a bicameral, or two-house, National Congress (Congreso de la Unión). The first house is the Senate (Cámara de Senadores), which has a total of 128 seats. Of these, 96 senators are directly elected by popular vote to serve six-year terms, and the remaining 32 seats are allocated on the basis of each party's popular vote.

The second house is the Federal Chamber of Deputies (Cámara Federal de Diputados), which has a total of 500 seats. Of these, 300 deputies are directly elected by popular vote to serve three-year terms. The remaining 200 seats are allocated for three-year terms, based on the popular vote of each party.

The judicial branch comprises a Supreme Court (Suprema Corte de Justicia), with judges appointed for life terms by the president after approval by the Senate. The court system includes twenty-one circuit courts and sixty-eight district courts throughout the country.

Each of Mexico's thirty-one states runs its own day-to-day affairs. Governors are elected to six-year terms and may not run for reelection. The state governments are further divided into city or town municipal governments called *municipios*. Each municipio has a president and a council that makes local laws.

THE LANGUAGES OF MEXICO

3

From Ancient Olmec to Modern Spanish

The long history of Mexico has resulted in a country with a diverse population. The population in 2001 was estimated to be just more than 101 million people. According to census reports, about 60 percent of the population is mestizo (Indian Spanish), 30 percent is Indian or predominately Indian, 9 percent is caucasian, and 1 percent is listed as "other."

Mestizos make up the largest percentage of the population. Mestizos are a blend of American Indian and Spanish ancestry. They trace their heritage back to the Indians who long inhabited Mexico and the Spaniards who came to Mexico after 1519. Most Mexicans think of themselves as mestizos, and their heritage is a matter of national pride. Almost all of Mexico's business leaders, politicians, and military leaders are mestizo.

Being considered an Indian in Mexico does not necessarily require a pure Indian ancestry. If a person lives in an Indian village, speaks an Indian language, or wears Indian clothes, he or she is considered to be an Indian even if the person is also a mestizo. Many different Indian groups still exist in Mexico today. There is great variation among the groups. In some cases, people from adjacent villages do not speak the same language or dialect. In many areas, Indian ways and customs are

Mexican muralist painter Diego Rivera (1886–1957) depicts the Tarascan people *(left)*, who inhabited the land around Rivera's birthplace of Guanajuato. Eight preconquest Mixtec codices created by the Oaxaca people exist today. This page *(above)* is part of the Codex Zouche Nuttall, which is housed in the British Museum in London. It was created between 1350 and 1500. The document depicts the birth, alliances, and conquests of several Mixtec rulers.

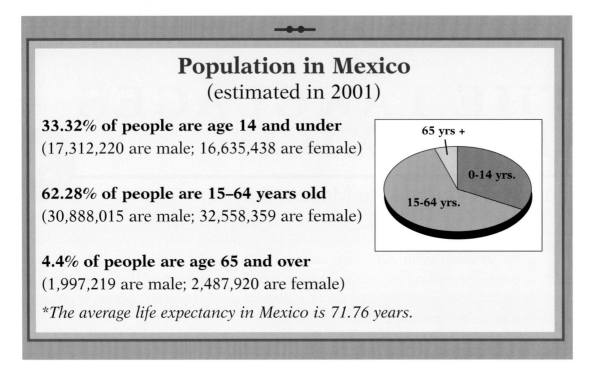

Population in Mexico
(estimated in 2001)

33.32% of people are age 14 and under
(17,312,220 are male; 16,635,438 are female)

62.28% of people are 15–64 years old
(30,888,015 are male; 32,558,359 are female)

4.4% of people are age 65 and over
(1,997,219 are male; 2,487,920 are female)

The average life expectancy in Mexico is 71.76 years.

still of primary importance in their lives. Many people wear traditional clothing, live in traditional-style houses, and use traditional methods to farm. Because of their numbers, the Indian groups still have great influence in Mexico today.

Although Spanish is the official language of Mexico, many people still use languages spoken by their ancestors. There are about sixty different languages and many dialects. About five million Mexicans, roughly 5 percent of the population, speak one of these native languages. Even with this diversity, it is estimated that almost 100 different languages have disappeared since the Spanish arrived in Mexico.

Maya

The Maya are probably the best known of all the Indian groups in Mexico and Central America. They built the great cities on the Yucatán Peninsula, in

This Mayan holy man makes offerings at his altar in the Yucatán Peninsula's rain forest. In Mayan culture and religion, each day, month, and year corresponded to a different god or goddess.

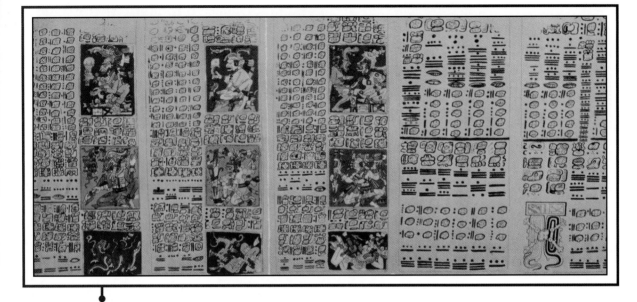

The Dresden Codex dates between 1200 and 1250. It is one of three codices to survive the book burning by Spanish clergy in 1521. Written by eight Mayan scribes, the Dresden Codex totals seventy-four pages that were folded accordion-style. They are painted on both sides.

Guatemala, and in Belize. They are known for having constructed tall pyramids and large, complex cities. During the classic period (AD 250 to 900), the Mayan civilization encompassed 120,000 square miles (311,000 square km). Today, Maya live in the same areas—the Yucatán Peninsula, Campeche, Tabasco, and Chiapas. Many speak one of twenty or more Mayan languages.

Today, the Maya live much the same as they did more than a thousand years ago. Their villages are made up of family groups. Each family group is close; several generations usually occupy the same house. The Maya raise corn, beans, and squash, as well as avocados, chili peppers, and sweet potatoes. In many areas, they hunt for small game to supplement their diet. Many of the Maya hold some of the same religious beliefs of their ancestors even though they have converted to one of the other Western religions.

Living in the highlands of Chiapas is a group of Maya known as the Lacondons. In their dialect of Maya, they call themselves the Hach Winik, or True People. The Lacandon live in the rain forest in Chiapas. Little is known about their exact roots, but some people believe they moved to the rain forest in Chiapas during the seventeenth or eighteenth century to escape the Spanish. They lived in small clans scattered throughout the rain forest and grew crops using the methods of the ancient Maya. The Lacondons performed the same religious ceremonies as their

Ruins at Monte Albán near Oaxaca were part of an ancient Zapotec capital, which dates back to 500 BC. It was one of the first cities in pre-Columbian ancient Mesoamerica, the areas south of the United States where advance cultures flowered. The stone stela located at this site is covered with Mixtec hieroglyphics.

ancestors did. By living in small groups in remote, unexplored parts of Mexico, they avoided detection by the rest of the world until the early twentieth century. There are only 400 to 500 Lacondon left today; they were relocated by the government to three villages. The forest they lived in for hundreds of years is now being used for timber.

Mixtec

The Mixtec Indians were an important group from about AD 900 until about 1520. The Mixtec established an empire in the mountains in the modern-day states of Guerrero, Oaxaca, and Puebla. They allied themselves with the Zapotec, but eventually were controlled by the Aztecs. The Mixtec were an important influence on the art of ancient Mexico. They produced a wide range of sophisticated arts and crafts, especially ceramics, jewelry, and small carvings of bone, clay, gold, jade, silver, turquoise, and wood. The Mixtec also created a number of codices, or historical books. Some of the surviving codices reveal intricate artwork as well as a history written in pictographs.

The Mixtec are still a large group in Mexico—an estimated 170,000 live in Oaxaca and Puebla today. Most are farmers and herders and speak their native language of Mixtec.

Made of beaten deerskin and lime wash, the Codex Fejérváry-Mayer is a pre-Columbian pictorial manuscript about the divining calendar and ceremonies devoted to the gods. It focuses on a sacred center and the god of fire, Xiuhtecuhtli.

Náhuatl

The Aztecs spoke a language called Náhuatl. Of all the Indian languages spoken in Mexico today, it is the most widely used. An estimated 1.5 million people speak Náhuatl. It is commonly spoken in parts of the Federal District and the states of Durango, México, Guerrero, Michoácan, Morelos, Oaxaca, Puebla, San Luís Potosi, Tabasco, Tlaxcala, and Veracruz.

In pre-Columbian times, Náhuatl was the common language among many of the Indian groups. When the Spaniards arrived in the 1500s, their Indian allies spoke Náhuatl, establishing a link between Mexican Spanish and Náhuatl. One result is that many places and things in Mexico have names that are Náhuatl or are derived from Náhuatl. Many of these words have also found their way into English. For example, the English words tomato, chocolate, and coyote are derived from the Náhuatl words *(xi)tomatl, xocolatl,* and *coyôtl.* Náhuatl words in Spanish usually have a suffix or ending of -tla, -tlan, -pa, -pan, -ca, -can, -c, -co, or -cingo.

A clay statue called The Scribe of Cuilapan, found at the ancient Zapotec site Quicopecua, was made between 200 BC and AD 200. The Mixtec writing on the chest and headdress reads "thirteen water and thirteen flint." The significance is unknown, although some archaeologists believe this describes a date.

Zapotec

The Zapotec Indians lived in the mountains of Oaxaca. Their civilization peaked between 1500 BC and AD 750. As the first civilization in Mexico to produce a written language, the Zapotec carved stories into stones, telling of conquests, sacrifices, and the neighboring tribes. The Zapotec people built large cities and temples in addition to smaller objects such as pottery. Around AD 750, the Zapotec people abandoned their capital of Monte Albán but maintained many smaller kingdoms, which were later conquered by the Aztecs. The rest eventually fell to the Spanish.

Today, several thousand remaining Zapotec Indians live in Oaxaca. They speak various dialects of the Zapotec language. Many continue to earn a living through farming, making pottery, or weaving. Their hand-crafted pottery and weavings are sold throughout Mexico and the world.

Spanish

Spanish is the official language of Mexico as well as Spain and most of Latin America. Worldwide, about 297 million people speak Spanish—about

Located fifty miles south of Mexico City, Cuernavaca is called the City of Eternal Spring because of its perfect climate and lush vegetation.

Some Useful Spanish Words

Hello	**Hola**	oh-la
Good morning	**Buenos días**	bway-nahs dee-as
Good afternoon	**Buenas tardes**	bway-nahs tar-days
Good night	**Buenas noches**	bway-nahs no-chays
Good-bye	**Adios**	ah-dee-os
Yes/No	**Si/No**	see/no
Please	**Por favor**	poor fa-vor
Thank you	**Gracias**	grah-see-us
Sorry!	**Lo siento**	low see-in-to
I don't know.	**No se**	no say
What is your name?	**¿Como se llama?**	co-mo say ya-ma
My name is. . .	**Mi nombre es. . .**	mee nom-bre ess. . .
I don't speak Spanish.	**No hablo español**	no ahb-lo es-pan-yol
Do you speak English?	**¿Hablas inglés?**	ahb-las een-gles
What time is it?	**¿Qué hora es?**	kay or-ah ess
Help me!	**Ayúdame**	eye-uda-may
I'm lost.	**Estoy perdido**	eh-stoy per-dee-doe
Where is. . . ?	**¿Dónde esta …?**	dohn-day ess-tah
House	**Casa**	cah-sah

Pronouncing Spanish Words

Spanish uses almost the same alphabet as English. In Spanish, there are fewer variations on the sounds of different letters and vowels. Once you learn the sound of each vowel and letter, pronouncing Spanish words is easy.

b and v	both are pronounced as the "b" in ball
s and z	both are pronounced as the "s" in sound
ch	is considered a letter and is pronounced like the "ch" in chair
ll	is called "elle" and is pronounced like the "y" in yes
ñ	is called "enye" and is pronounced "nyah"
a	is always pronounced "ah," as in hat
e	is always pronounced "eh," as in wet
i	is always pronounced "ee," as in seen (but shorter)
o	is always pronounced "oh," as in cot
u	is always pronounced "oo," as in food

one-third live in Mexico. Dialects and pronunciation are different between the Old World and the New World. In Spain, the people speak Castilian Spanish. In Latin America, people speak American Spanish. While the two types of Spanish are similar, there are differences in their vocabularies and pronunciations. In Mexico, no matter what kind of Spanish they speak, people tend to understand each other very well.

Along the promenade called Malecón in Puerto Vallarta, tourists view the sights from a trolley as it travels the mile-long seawall walkway that stretches the length of the city.

The Spanish spoken in Mexico is sometimes indirect. People often use vague terms to avoid causing trouble or showing commitment. Many words have double meanings. Some of these double meanings may be subtle and not recognized by someone who is not fluent in Spanish. Mexicans consider it rude to use language with excessive frankness or directness. Even serious conversations are usually preceded with small talk about family or friends.

In Spanish, verbs have two forms—formal and informal. Formal verbs are used to show respect for someone. Formal forms of verbs are used when talking

A woman sells magazines in Chetumal, Mexico. Although Mexico is the world's largest Spanish-speaking country, it is linguistically diverse with sixty-two other living indigenous languages spoken. A living language is one that is spoken every day.

with elders, teachers, policemen, bosses, or anyone else who has your respect. Friends use the informal verb forms when they chat among themselves.

In Mexico, the verb *esperar* means "to expect." However, the same verb also means "to await" and "to hope." The true meaning of these different definitions of the verb esperar may become clear if one is in a rural area waiting for a bus. At first, the bus is expected to come, but as time passes and the bus does not arrive, that expectation changes to hope that the bus will come.

Spanish in Mexico is also full of slang terms, which often have double meanings. Sometimes it is difficult for a foreigner to understand exactly what a Mexican means. Slang also varies from region to region. The slang terms used in one region may have a totally different meaning in another region. A visitor to Mexico who uses slang terms correctly has learned to understand Mexican Spanish.

In general, Mexicans are happy when foreigners try to use Spanish. Mexicans are polite and patient people and will often help the speaker. They may drive the conversation in such a way that the foreigner can express what he or she wants, and when the foreigner does not know a particular word, the Mexican will help him or her. Also, Mexicans are not deeply offended when a foreigner mangles their language by mixing verbs. This is one of the ways that Mexicans show their generous nature.

Nicknames

Mexican people often have nicknames. Some nicknames are standardized. For example, someone named Francisco may be called Pancho, and someone named Antonio may be called Toño. Other times, a person might have a nickname that describes his or her appearance or something that happened to him or her. These nicknames are used as terms of endearment and are not considered rude.

This poster advertises a spa in Ixtapan de la Sal. Its warm thermal waters are purported to have curative qualities. Although the water appears dirty as a result of the high mineral content, the baths are said to heal arthritic and rheumatic conditions.

47

MEXICAN MYTHS AND LEGENDS

4

Throughout Mexico's long history, myths and legends have influenced the customs and culture of the people. Myths and legends range from simple stories to epic adventures. Many of the tales from the ancient Mexican civilizations are still told today. Some have been passed down through oral tradition from generation to generation, while others were written in ancient languages or illustrated in other ways.

The Mayan Creation Myth

Almost every culture has a myth that describes the creation of its people. This is true of the Maya. The myth was written down during the sixteenth century, although the story is much older than the written manuscript. The story, called the Popol Vuh, was recorded in the Quiche dialect of Maya but written using Roman characters. From the peak of the Mayan civilization, people have used illustrations from the story of Popol Vuh to decorate pottery. The Popol Vuh starts at the beginning of time.

According to the story, there were three failed attempts to create the Mayan people. Each time there

A shrine of the Virgin of Guadalupe *(left)* is located near the Seri Indian village of Punta Chueca. The last 200 pure-blooded Seri Indians live here, in northern Mexico. Dominican Father Francisco Ximénez wrote the *Treasure of the Three Languages (above)* between 1700 and 1703. A minister in Guatemala, he used a combination of Indian languages and Spanish to write and translate a number of books, including the Popol Vuh, the Mayan creation story. The book includes the Ten Commandments, Beatitudes, prayers, and information about early Central American people.

The Creation

Here is the story of the beginning,
when there was not one bird,
not one fish,
not one mountain.
Here is the sky, all alone.
Here is the sea, all alone.
There is nothing more—
no sound, no movement.
Only the sky and the sea.
Only Heart-of-Sky, alone.
And these are his names:
Maker and Modeler,
Kukulkan, and Hurricane.
But there is no one to speak his names.
There is no one to praise his glory.
There is no one to nurture his greatness.

—Popol Vuh

was a fatal flaw. It was not until the fourth try that the Maya were created. The story tells of the Hero Twins who enter Xibalba, the Mayan underworld. They have a series of adventures and play the sacred ball game with the gods found in Xibalba. Through luck and trickery, the Hero Twins defeat the gods, and hope is given to mankind. The sacred ball game was played with a hard rubber ball that was knocked through a stone hoop set high up on the wall of a court.

Quetzalcóatl

Quetzalcóatl (the feathered serpent) is the Náhuatl name for an especially important god. Quetzalcóatl is identified with the air and the wind. While he is not the most powerful god, Quetzalcóatl is probably the most widely known, making his way into many aspects of everyday Mayan life. He is associated with many gods, and he also appears in myths by himself. Although Quetzalcóatl did not have any particular power or action, like the rain god or the thunder god, he is included in the stories of almost all of the Indian groups of Mexico. Quetzalcóatl had many names, such as Gukumatz, Nine

This shell mosaic dates from the early post-classic period and depicts Quetzalcóatl rising from the jaws of the earth as represented by the coyote. According to Aztec myth, Quetzalcóatl was supposed to return from the east and reclaim his power. However, the Aztec Indians tragically mistook Cortés for him.

Winds, and Kukulkan. One of the most important predictions made by Quetzalcóatl was that he would return to Mexico from the east and reclaim power from all the Indians. When Cortés arrived in Mexico from the east with horses, armor, and guns, the Indians believed he might be Quetzalcóatl. The uncertainty made it easier for Cortés to conquer the Indians with his small army.

Another myth involving Quetzalcóatl tells how the Toltecs got chocolate. Quetzalcóatl came down from the heavens, bringing a small tree to the Toltecs. He said he had stolen the tree from his brother and that it was a gift to the Toltecs. Quetzalcóatl planted the tree and told them that it would grow chocolate. When the tree grew flowers and then brown pods, he picked the pods and dried them. He taught the women how to roast and grind the pods. He instructed the Toltecs to mix the pods with hot water and hot peppers to make a bitter drink. As time passed, they added honey to the bitter drink. By the time the Spaniards arrived, the Toltecs were mixing the roasted and ground chocolate with milk and sugar. To the Toltecs, this is how the gods gave them their sacred chocolate drink.

The Poinsettia

Some of the myths and legends of the Mexicans, such as the story of the poinsettia plant, are more recent. The poinsettia, now familiar around the world, is a plant with brilliant red leaves that appear from late November to early December. Poinsettias grow wild in Mexico, but according to this legend, they did not always turn red at Christmas. According to the story, a young girl named Pepita, who was very poor, had nothing to offer the Christ child at the Christmas services. Having no gift made her sad. So on her way to church, she picked some flowering weeds. When she got to the church, she made her way to the front and placed the bouquet on altar. When the weeds turned a brilliant red color, everyone in the church witnessed the Christmas miracle. From

Aztecs first discovered poinsettias in the tropical region of Taxco, near Cuernavaca, and brought the plant to their highlands for cultivation. The poinsettia was prized by the pre-Hispanic people because of the curative properties of the milk that dripped from the leaves and stem when cut.

that day forward, it is said, poinsettias have turned bright red at Christmas. They are known as flores de Nochebuena (flowers of Christmas Eve).

The new Basilica of Guadalupe, completed in 1976, houses the old basilica from 1709.

The Legend of Juan Diego

Some legends in Mexico are the basis for religious beliefs and holidays. The legend of Juan Diego, considered a miracle in Mexico, underlies Mexicans' great faith in the Virgin Mary. According to the story, the Virgin Mary appeared four times to a poor Indian peasant named Juan Diego. She appeared first on December 9, 1531, near Mexico City, at a place called Tepeyac Hill. The Virgin Mary asked Juan Diego to go to the bishop of Mexico and tell him to build a church on Tepeyac Hill dedicated to her.

Juan Diego went to the bishop, but the bishop did not believe Juan Diego's story. Juan Diego returned to the hill and asked the Virgin Mary to select someone else who was more worthy to perform her task. On her fourth visit with Juan Diego on December 12, the Virgin Mary took Juan Diego to the top of the hill and picked flowers for him to give to the bishop. She wrapped the flowers in Juan Diego's cloak. When Juan Diego

delivered the flowers to the bishop, he opened his cloak and instead of flowers the cloak revealed an elaborate portrait of the Virgin Mary. This was considered a miracle.

The bishop approved the construction of the Basilica of the Virgin on Tepeyac Hill in Mexico City. Still a major pilgrimage site, it attracts people from all over the world who come to be healed there. On December 12 each year, a celebration is held at the basilica where the elaborate portrait from the cloak of Juan Diego is framed and hangs. December 12 is a holiday in Mexico, celebrating the Virgin of Guadalupe, Mexico's patron saint.

Some Scary Legends

Some legends are told as a way to scare people into behaving properly. Almost every culture worldwide has some type of scary figure to help keep children in line. In Mexico, the legend of La Llorona (The Crying Woman) has been passed from generation to generation and has taken many forms. The legend describes a woman named María who is shunned by her true love because she has two children. She decides to drown her children in a river to win the affections of her true love, but the plan fails. María kills herself and becomes a ghost, wandering Mexico's riverbanks, while wailing, crying, and searching for her dead children. According to the legend, La Llorona may snatch children who misbehave.

Another legend that has circulated widely in Mexico, all over Latin America, and even through parts of the United States is the legend of a beast called the *chupacabras* (literally meaning "goat sucker"). According to the legend, the chupacabras is responsible for killing livestock and drinking their blood. The chupacabras is usually described as having a reptilian body, an oval head, bulging red eyes, fanged teeth, and a long, darting tongue. The chupacabras only hunts at night. Although sightings have been reported many times, it has never been captured. The chupacabras was first reported in Puerto Rico during the 1960s. Since that time, sightings and stories of the chupacabras have spread throughout Latin America and Mexico. Maybe one day, someone will catch a chupacabras, and the mystery will be solved.

Cardinal Norberto Rivera, archbishop of Mexico City, officiates mass at the new Basilica of Guadalupe on the twenty-fourth anniversary of Pope John Paul II's installment as the 265th pope of the Catholic Church. Above him hangs the original image of the Virgin of Guadalupe.

MEXICAN FESTIVALS AND CEREMONIES OF ANTIQUITY AND TODAY

Mexico has a long tradition of festivals or fiestas. Every day there is a fiesta somewhere. Some fiestas are national events, while others take place in one region or in a single village.

Carnaval

Carnaval is the celebration that takes place before the beginning of Catholic Lent. It gives Catholics one last chance to enjoy guilty pleasures before the forty days of Lent. During Lent, devout Catholics give up eating meat as well as other pleasant activities. Carnaval runs for five days, ending on Ash Wednesday. The celebration of Lent ends on Easter Sunday.

Carnaval is popular in some parts of Mexico. In Mazatlán, Carnaval attracts about 300,000 people from all over the world. Mazatlán's celebration of Carnaval is the third largest in the world, behind Rio de Janeiro and New Orleans. Carnaval is also popular in Ensenada, La Paz, and Veracruz.

A huge celebration enjoyed by people young and old, Carnaval is a joyous party. People celebrate with decorated floats, parades, costumes, music, and dancing. Vendors sell food, drinks, snacks, and crafts. Live bands and stereos provide music. People of all ages enjoy the tradition of cracking *cascarones* (confetti-filled eggshells) over each other's heads. Some towns organize festivals and fairs complete with carnival-type

On the Day of the Dead, a man stands among graves that have been decorated with candles and flowers *(left)*. During the Day of the Dead, family members gather for festive graveside reunions. People perform in mariachi bands. They bring food in picnic baskets and drink tequila to celebrate the dead. Children *(above)* are dressed for Carnaval.

rides. Larger cities often have elaborate fireworks displays. All the action, excitement, and parties peak on the weekend and wind down on Fat Tuesday. On Ash Wednesday, all Catholics go to church for services that usher in the beginning of Lent.

Semana Santa

Semana Santa (Holy Week) runs from Palm Sunday to Easter Sunday and is widely celebrated by Catholics. For the entire week, many businesses close and people take vacations to be with family and friends. Aside from masses at church, there are many other activities. Unlike Carnaval, Semana Santa is more somber. Throughout Mexico, the holiday is observed differently, with each region adding something unique to its celebration.

During Semana Santa, Catholic churches often have important religious items on display as well as traditional altars for offerings and candles. People build altars at their homes and businesses. They decorate the city streets and their houses. In some areas, the Catholic Church organizes processions, where penitents (believers who are sorry for their sins) follow floats depicting Jesus. The penitents follow the float, sometimes walking and sometimes crawling. Some villages reenact the journey of Jesus with characters dressed in costume. The characters include Roman soldiers, Jesus, and his followers. The activities of Semana Santa end after mass on Easter Sunday.

Cinco de Mayo

Cinco de Mayo (May 5) is a celebration to commemorate the defeat of the French army at the Battle of Puebla in 1862. Cinco de Mayo is extremely popular in the state of Puebla. In other parts of Mexico, Cinco de Mayo is celebrated but with less fervor. Cinco de Mayo is becoming a popular celebration along the United States–Mexico border and is gaining importance in U.S. cities that have large Mexican populations. Celebrated with food, drinks, music, and dancing, Cinco de Mayo is often confused with Mexican Independence Day, which falls on September 16.

Mexican Independence Day

Mexican Independence Day is celebrated on September 16 with food, drinks, music, and dancing. Some cities have fairs and picnics, and some have fireworks displays. The festivities begin at about 11 PM on September 15 with an official reading of *El Grito de Dolores* (The cry of Dolores) at midnight. On Mexican Independence Day, people recognize Mexico's call for independence from Spain in 1810, even though the country did not win its independence until 1821.

Men watch the Cinco de Mayo parade, which celebrates the victory of 4,000 Mexican soldiers who defeated the French and traitor Mexican army of 8,000 at the Battle of Puebla.

Día de los Muertos

Día de los Muertos (Day of the Dead) is a mix of Native Mexican and European traditions. Dating back to the time of the Aztecs, a celebration was held to honor the dead. In the Catholic religion, November 1 (All Saints' Day) and November 2 (All Souls' Day) also honor the dead. Since the sixteenth century, these two occasions have merged into one.

Once recognized throughout Mexico, Día de los Muertos is now observed mainly in southern Mexico. The celebration usually begins on the evening of October 31. It is not a sad or somber event. Instead, it is more like a happy fiesta during which people celebrate relatives who have died. Houses and cemeteries are decorated with flowers, plants, and statues of skeletons. For the living, Día de los Muertos is celebrated with *pan de muerto*, a rich cake with meringue frosting made to look like bones, as well as skull-shaped candies and papier-mâché skeletons. Ceremonies performed at cemeteries include burning *copal* (an incense), praying, chanting, and lighting candles. Afterward, food and drinks are served in a party-like atmosphere.

Mexico celebrated the 192nd anniversary of its independence from Spain on September 16, 2002. As part of the Independence Day festivities, President Vicente Fox Quesada rode on horseback through the town of Dolores.

Sugar skulls, a traditional folk art from southern Mexico, adorn altars to welcome back dead spirits of loved ones during the Day of the Dead.

On All Saints' Day, deceased children are remembered; relatives decorate their graves with toys and colorful balloons. Deceased adults are honored on All Souls' Day with offerings of food, drinks, personal possessions, and flowers.

Día de Nuestra Señora de Guadalupe

Día de Nuestra Señora de Guadalupe (Day of Our Lady of Guadalupe) is celebrated on December 12, the feast day of the Virgin Mary, patron saint of Mexico. In 1531, the Virgin Mary appeared to Indian peasant Juan Diego and asked that a church be built in her honor, which the bishop of Mexico City did after witnessing a miracle. This day draws millions of worshipers each year to the Basilica of the Virgin in Mexico City to give thanks for answering their prayers. Many worshipers, young and old, crawl up Tepeyac Hill on their hands and knees in penance and to offer thanks. Surrounding the basilica, the celebration rages on with Indians in traditional costumes, food, drinks, visitors, and vendors. Aside from the Vatican in Rome, the Basilica of the Virgin is the most visited Catholic site in the world.

Navidad

Navidad (Christmas) is an important observance in Mexico. Most people take off two weeks around Christmas to celebrate. Navidad begins with Las Posadas (the inns) processions that represent the search Joseph and Mary made in Bethlehem for a place to stay. People dressed as Joseph and Mary ride a donkey and wander around town with a choir of children asking for a place to stay. As the procession travels through town, everyone turns them away until they reach a prearranged house where they are accepted. Then the fiesta begins. Traditional food and drinks are served. Piñatas, vessels that have been filled with tiny candies and toys and decorated with brightly colored papier-mâché and ribbons, are available for the kids. The piñatas are made to resemble animals or other characters. Children wearing blindfolds take turns hitting the piñata with a stick

Mexicans parade through the streets to celebrate the Virgin of Guadalupe in front of the Basilica of Guadalupe in Mexico City. The Day of Our Lady of Guadalupe is one of the most important religious holidays in Mexico. Young boys and girls are chosen to represent Juan Diego and the Virgin. They wear traditional native dress for this celebration.

until it breaks open. Then the kids scramble for the treats.

La Nochebuena (Christmas Eve) is a time to celebrate and attend Catholic mass at midnight. Some towns have dances on the *zocalo* (town square). Unlike the custom of exchanging gifts on Christmas Day in the United States, Mexicans exchange gifts on January 6. This day, called Día de los Santos Reyes (King's Day, or Epiphany), represents the day that the three wise men visited the baby Jesus and offered presents.

Fiestas and Special Events

Mexico has a long tradition of fiestas or celebrations. In fact, it is sometimes called the land of fiestas. Almost every day, there is a fiesta somewhere in Mexico. Some fiestas are national events while others take place in only one region or in a single village. Not all fiestas are happy celebrations. Some fiestas are somber and deeply reverent. Some fiestas last only one or two days while others may last for a week or longer.

Ancient Events

Before the arrival of the Spanish, many people of the ancient civilizations in Mexico celebrated special events with human sacrifices and the eating of human flesh. According to historians, the Aztecs sacrificed hundreds, sometimes thousands of captives in a single day during their special events. Today, these practices have been replaced with costumes, music, and food.

THE RELIGIONS OF MEXICO THROUGHOUT ITS HISTORY

6

Religion was an important aspect of the pre-Columbian civilizations of Mexico. Religion guided all aspects of life, especially agriculture and government. After Cortés arrived in Mexico, the Catholic Church built missions expecting to convert the Indians to Catholicism. Today, about 89 percent of all Mexicans are Catholic; the remaining 11 percent belong to other religions.

The Maya

The Maya worshiped more than 300 gods and goddesses, each of whom ruled an aspect of everyday life. Some of the most important figures were Chac (the rain god), Kinich Ahau (the sun god), and Ix Chel (the moon goddess).

The Maya built temples in their cities. The temples were on large platforms or

The wooden statue *(left)* depicts the Aztec rain god, Tlaloc, to whom offerings were made to ask for rain clouds and fertility. The headdress of Tlaloc indicates his high rank among the gods. The illustration *(above)* shows the rain god Chac (sometimes Chaac) from a Mayan codex, which dates to AD 900.

Mayan Calendar

The Maya developed a complex calendar system that consisted of eighteen months of twenty days each. At the end of the year, there were five additional days. Each day of the Mayan calendar had a special religious importance and was dedicated to one of the gods or goddesses. The Maya made offerings of corn, other foodstuffs, or valuable items to their gods and goddesses. Additional offerings were made in the form of sacrifices. The Maya sacrificed small animals as well as people. Those who were chosen to be sacrificed were sometimes given a place of great honor; the Maya also sacrificed captives from wars.

atop tall pyramids. Priests performed ceremonies that were held either in private or with large audiences. Altars were often constructed in caves because the underworld, called Xibalba, was the home to many gods and goddesses. Every house had a small altar that the family would use for private ceremonies.

The Maya believed strongly in an afterlife. When a person died, he or she was buried with personal belongings that were needed in the next world. The dead were usually wrapped in cloth or painted red and buried with their belongings under the floors of their houses. When leaders died, they were buried in pyramids or temples with many offerings,

Mayan hieroglyphs of animals representing blocks of time are carved into limestone. Gods stand for numbers. These days and numbers represent February 11, AD 526, in our calendar.

Dating from the late classic period between 600 and 900, this Mayan sacrificial altar is located in front of the Temple of the Labyrinth. Loss and rebirth were themes celebrated by the Maya rituals of human sacrifice.

including valued objects and pottery vessels filled with corn. Sometimes, servants would be sacrificed and placed inside the tomb to accompany their leader into the next world.

Today, many of the Maya in Mexico have converted to Catholicism or one of the other Western religions. However, many of the Maya still perform ancient ceremonies for special events such as planting crops, harvesting crops, to ask for rain, or to request luck, health, or general blessings.

The Aztecs

To the Aztecs, like the Maya, religion was extremely important. The Aztecs worshiped hundreds of gods and goddesses, who they believed ruled over every aspect of their world and lives. Because the Aztecs depended on agriculture, they believed that the gods and

The sacred city of Chichén Itzá, where hundreds of buildings once stood, was one of the most important sites of the Mayan culture. Kukulcan's Pyramid, seen here, is a square-based stepped pyramid, built as an astrological calendar. One Mexican researcher has suggested that this pyramid was connected to agricultural rituals.

This illustration from a sixteenth-century codex depicts Aztec priests cutting out the heart of a youth as a sacrifice to the sun god. The most common form of Aztec human sacrifice was the removal of the heart.

goddesses controlled specific aspects of crops. One important god was Tláloc, who ruled rain and fertility. Other important gods were Centéotl, the corn god; Xipe Tótec, the god of springtime and regrowth; and Quetzalcóatl, the feathered serpent, the god associated with civilization and learning. Many ceremonies were held for these and other goods.

Human sacrifice was an important part of many Aztec ceremonies. The Aztecs sacrificed captives from the wars they fought with neighboring tribes. The most common method of sacrifice was to split open the victim's chest and remove the heart. Most sacrifices took place in temples at the ceremonial centers of the city. Temples were constructed of a solid stair-stepped bases with small platforms on top. Each temple was dedicated to a specific god. Ceremonial centers had living quarters for priests, sacred pools for ceremonial

Carved in 1479, the Aztec calendar, Stone of the Sun, kept track of two different aspects of time. The Aztecs counted the days for religious purposes. They kept track of the years, based on a 365 solar count calendar, for the agricultural and ceremonial calendar of the state.

cleansing, and racks for holding the skulls of sacrificial victims.

The Arrival of the Catholic Church

When Cortés arrived in Mexico, he brought with him missionaries from the Catholic Church. As Cortés and his army formed allies and conquered the Indian groups, priests and other members of the Catholic Church set about to convert them. Although many Indians converted to Catholicism, many did not. Those who did not convert died at the hands of the Spanish.

The Catholic Church claimed huge tracts of land in Mexico and built missions and churches. The land-wealthy Catholic Church became very powerful and controlled much of the politics. In spite of the power and influence of the Catholic Church, many of the converted Indians continued to practice their ancient beliefs as well as those of their newfound religion.

During the colonial period, the Catholic Church was closely linked to the government—which protected the Catholic Church by prohibiting other religious groups from entering Mexico.

By the mid-1800s, around the time of Mexico's independence from Spain, there was a separation

The Aztec Calendars

The Aztecs had two calendars. One was a religious calendar with 260 days, in which each day had a special religious significance. The Aztecs also had a calendar system similar to that of the Maya, which had eighteen months of twenty days and five special days at the end. The Aztec calendars followed fifty-two year cycles. Every fifty-two years, the two calendars began again. Special ceremonies marked the event.

A young girl prays at an altar of Our Lady of Guadalupe. When Catholic missionaries arrived in Mexico, they taught the Indians to read Spanish, Latin, and music. They converted many of them to the Catholic religion.

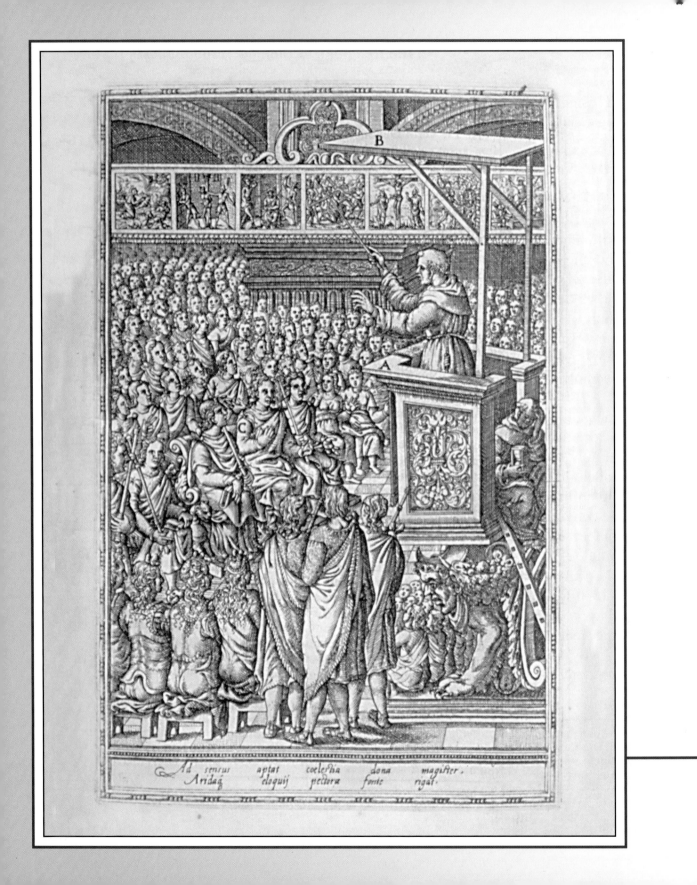

Ad sensus aptat coelestia dona magister.
Aridaǫ eloquij pectora fonte rigat.

Housed in the Biblioteca Nacional in Madrid, Spain, an illustration dated 1522 depicts Indian slaves laying the foundation for the cathedral in Mexico City. After Cortés conquered the Aztec Empire, he founded Mexico City. It was built on the ruins of Tenochtitlán. The European-style colonial capital was constructed with the rubble from destroyed Aztec structures.

between the Catholic Church and the government. The government passed laws prohibiting the church from owning lands and taking part in politics. Because of corruption and the church's continuing power, these laws were not always applied equally. As the power of the Catholic Church lessened, other religious groups began to enter Mexico.

Between the 1500s and the mid-1800s, the Catholic Church controlled most of the schools in Mexico. This served to reinforce its power until the mid-1800s, when the government and the Catholic Church separated. At that time, the schools became the responsibility of the government.

The Catholic Church Today

Today, the Catholic Church is still a powerful force in Mexico. However, even with 89 percent of the population practicing Catholicism, other religious groups are beginning to gain power. In the past fifty years, the number of Protestants in Mexico has grown rapidly. Even among Catholics, the number of people attending mass is decreasing. Against the doctrine of the Catholic Church, divorce is becoming accepted and common. People are using birth control, and abortions are available. Even with the erosion of basic Catholic beliefs and dropping attendance, the influence of the Catholic Church remains strong in Mexico.

A 1579 copper engraving by artist Diego de Valadés from his book *Rethorica Christiana* shows a Franciscan monk preaching to Indians. Franciscan monks arrived in Mexico in 1524 to convert the Indians to Catholicism.

THE ART AND ARCHITECTURE OF MEXICO

7

The Olmecs were the first people in Mexico to make great advances in both art and architecture. The civilizations that followed continued to refine and redefine art and architecture throughout Mexico. When the Spanish arrived, they brought a European tradition, which added to the mix. Today, Mexico's art and architecture continue to show influences from their earliest pre-Columbian civilizations and the Spanish colonial period, as well as many contemporary cultures from other parts of the world.

The Olmecs

The Olmec civilization was the first in Mexico to use pyramids as an architectural style. The Olmecs were also the first to create detailed stone carvings. With large stone heads, many weighing several tons, the statues may give a realistic view of what an Olmec person looked like. One of the oldest established pre-Columbian traditions is that of making fine pottery and jewelry. The Olmecs carved jade into beads and ornaments. Like other pre-Columbian civilizations, the Olmecs performed these tasks without the aid of metal tools.

The colossal head *(above)*, sculpted by the Olmecs, has similar features to the Olmec warrior king: the flattened nose, wide lips, and capping headpiece. Statues such as this were carved from volcanic stone. A statue of Chac Mool *(left)*, meaning Red Claw, who is believed to be the Mayan messenger to the gods, reclines in front of the Temple of the Warriors at the archaeological site Chichén Itzá. He holds a receptacle for Mayan offerings.

El Castillo, located at Chichén Itzá, an ancient Mayan city, has 365 steps leading to the top platform. With one step for each day of the year, this is evidence that the temple was linked to the Mayan calendar. It was also built on the solar equinox with a snake's head at the bottom of the staircase. When the equinox hits, the stairs reflect light so it looks like a snake is coming from the heavens.

The Maya

The Maya borrowed their basic architectural style from the Olmecs but added many innovations to create a unique style. Tall pyramids, reaching as high as 130 feet (40 m), were built to represent sacred mountains. The Maya topped the pyramids with thatched-roof temples. Also, they constructed lavish palaces and stone buildings, shaping rocks into blocks and fitting them together to form the outside shell of a building. Once in place, workers smoothed the blocks with stucco and painted them. Red was a popular color. On the inside of many temples, artists created large murals. Many of the buildings were decorated with elaborate stucco masks representing different gods. Some Mayan buildings had high arched ceilings that made small rooms feel more spacious. Over time, the Maya reshaped and enlarged the existing buildings. Often they covered over an old building, adding a new rock and stucco exterior. Many of the Mayan cities lasted hundreds of years. Because each addition is preserved underneath, archaeologists can establish a complete record of a building's history.

The Maya also undertook incredible construction projects such as building *sacbes*, or raised stone roads. Some sacbes extended for many kilometers, connecting each city and important ceremonial locations. The Maya also used their skills to drain swamps to be used for agricultural purposes, to terrace the land, and to build cities in the jungle.

A Mayan fresco painted on limestone at Bonampak, a classic period Mayan site. It depicts Maya raiding a village to capture prisoners for the ritual of human sacrifice. Murals at Bonampak provided the first evidence that the Maya waged war on their neighbors.

The Maya also excelled at art, fashioning incredible limestone carvings that tell stories of religious events, rulers, and war. The writings on these stone carvings are still being deciphered today.

In addition to carving, the Maya painted elaborate scenes on pieces of pottery that were formed into a variety of shapes, including bowls, platters, plates, dishes, jars, and ceremonial figurines. Skilled at carving jade, they made tubular and round beads, and carved figurines and other shapes. Many of these artworks have lasted to this day. An excellent example of Maya handiwork can be seen at the temple in Bonampak in the Yucatán Peninsula.

The Aztecs

The Aztecs built cities in much the same style as other pre-Columbian civilizations. The Aztec capital city of Tenochtitlán is a huge monument to their religion. Large pyramids and palace complexes built out of carved stone blocks and decorated with macabre images of skulls and sacrifices are scattered throughout the city. Within the city, which was surrounded by walls, was an elaborate system of roads and streets. When the Spanish first arrived at Tenochtitlán, they were amazed at its complexity.

Capítulo 5.º

De como los Mexicanos avisados de
su Dios fuéron á vuscar el Tunal y
el Aguila, y como lo hallaron, y del
acuerdo que para el edificio tubiéron

Otro dia de mañana el Sacerdote
Quauhtloquetzqui, cuidadoso de rebelar la re

This Aztec *cuauhxicalli*, or eagle bowl, was at one time used for storing the hearts from human sacrifices. Five priests performed the sacrificial ceremony, four to hold the victim and one to cut out the heart. While the victim was still alive, the heart would be removed using a flint knife.

The Aztecs were skilled at working with gold, and they made figures and jewelry out of this valuable material. Unfortunately, the Spanish took much of their gold and melted it into ingots before they shipped it off to Spain. The Aztecs also made elaborate stone sculptures. The most familiar of all Aztec sculptures are the round representations of the Aztec calendar.

The Spanish Colonial Period

When the Spanish conquistadors arrived in Mexico, they came to conquer as well as to colonize Mexico. Priests and other members of the Catholic Church arrived with the conquistadors; they came to convert the Indians to the Catholic religion. The Catholic missionaries began building missions as the Spanish officials began building a new government. Missions, buildings, and homes were constructed in a style known as Spanish colonial. Built from the mid-1500s to the late 1700s, the Spanish colonial style is characterized by simple, functional construction with durable materials. Most of the buildings were massive because they also served to protect the colonists against Indian raids. The doors were often plain, thick wood. During the 1600s, intricate and ornate carvings were added to the buildings, and influences from the native Indians were often incorporated into the designs. By the 1700s, the style had grown to one with richly ornate columns and alternating curves and angles. This style is still visible in the larger churches throughout Mexico, with the

A fifteenth-century Spanish drawing from a manuscript about the ancient history of New Spain recounts the Aztec founding of Tenochtitlán, where an eagle clutched a serpent. Today, the eagle and serpent are Mexico's national symbols.

Santo Domingo Church in Oaxaca, built in 1576, has served as the seat of the Dominican order since the sixteenth century. This church, built with a combination of Renaissance, baroque, and gothic ornamentation, is the best-preserved example of colonial religious architecture in Mexico.

best example being the cathedral in Mexico City. Buildings created during the Spanish colonial period are very sturdy. Not only are many of these centuries-old buildings still standing in many Mexican cities, but many are still in use today.

The Haciendas

Haciendas (large land estates) first appeared shortly after the conquest of Mexico. Haciendas began as land grants of a few hundred acres that were given to conquistadors as a reward for their services. The headquarters of the hacienda was typically a large house built in Spanish colonial style. In addition to serving as the headquarters, it was also a small fortress. The exterior of the building was plain, with thick walls and shuttered windows. The interior reflected Spanish and Moorish influence with highly decorated colorful tile work, fountains, arched passageways, and large open areas. More and more haciendas were established in Mexico, and the size of the lands they controlled increased. The haciendas continued to exist until the Mexican Revolution of 1910

when much of the land was taken away from the owners by the government. Today, many of the hacienda houses still exist and are still owned by the original families. Some haciendas are still used as houses and ranch headquarters, while others have been converted into small hotels.

Hacienda is a Spanish word with a Latin root meaning "things to do." Historically, a hacienda was the most prominent building on a Mexican estate or plantation. It functioned as the center of family activity. Over the years, haciendas have evolved into contemporary buildings. But they still retain the Spanish and southwestern flavor of Mexico.

Mexico City—An Architectural Showcase

Mexico City is one of the largest urban areas in the world. A visit there reveals a chaotic mix of streets crowded with people and vendors, traffic jams, and more buildings than can be counted. It is hard to believe that at one time, Mexico City was a model of urban development. Mexico City was originally designed to be the "City of Palaces," with uniform buildings reflecting the best ideas of European design schools of the day. Today, Mexico City has examples of all the styles of architecture used in Mexico.

Mexico City was first established on top of the ruins of Tenochtitlán. The original design for the city called for two main boulevards, one running from east to west and the other running north to south from a great central plaza. All streets were to follow a grid pattern based on the two main boulevards. The first buildings were constructed following the Spanish colonial style. As in the rest of Mexico, this style was popular until the late 1700s, when the first architectural school opened in Mexico. As a result, the designs for new buildings began to reflect a strong neoclassical influence, which was popular in Europe at that time. Neoclassical architecture is characterized by large buildings with Greek-style columns.

After the War of Independence in 1810, the neoclassical style of architecture was replaced by President Porfirio Díaz's vision of turning Mexico City into the City of Palaces. A large number of Europeans were moving to Mexico City during that period of time, and the building designs were borrowed from styles used in France, Spain, Germany, and other European countries.

After the revolution of 1910, Mexico City returned to its roots with a unique style called neocolonialism. Building designs, featuring colonial styling and new materials, were also influenced by European architecture of the period. Mexican architecture of today reflects influences of many of the popular trends in European architecture from the past 100 years. Mexico City showcases a unique history of architectural styles of the past 450 years.

Famous Artists of Mexico

Best known for their traditional Indian designs and religious art, Mexican painters did not receive much attention until Gerardo Murillo began to paint. Known as Dr. Atl, Murillo was born in Guadalajara in 1875. He studied art at the Fine Arts Academy in Mexico City. Given a grant to study art in Europe, Murillo was influenced strongly by the art styles of the time. He returned to Mexico in 1903. By 1910, Murillo had created a new art medium called Atlcolors, a type of paint that is still used today. Using Atlcolors, he painted the first modern murals in Mexico. Murillo's paintings were popular, and he continued to work, taking part in politics, throughout the Mexican Revolution. Murillo taught art; some of his students have become Mexico's best-known artists. Murillo died in 1964, but he left a great legacy in the Mexican art world.

Located in the patio corridor of the National Palace in Mexico City is Diego Rivera's 1945 mural, *The Great City of Tenochtitlán*. This piece was part of a larger mural depicting the history of Mexico. It was left unfinished when Rivera died on November 25, 1957.

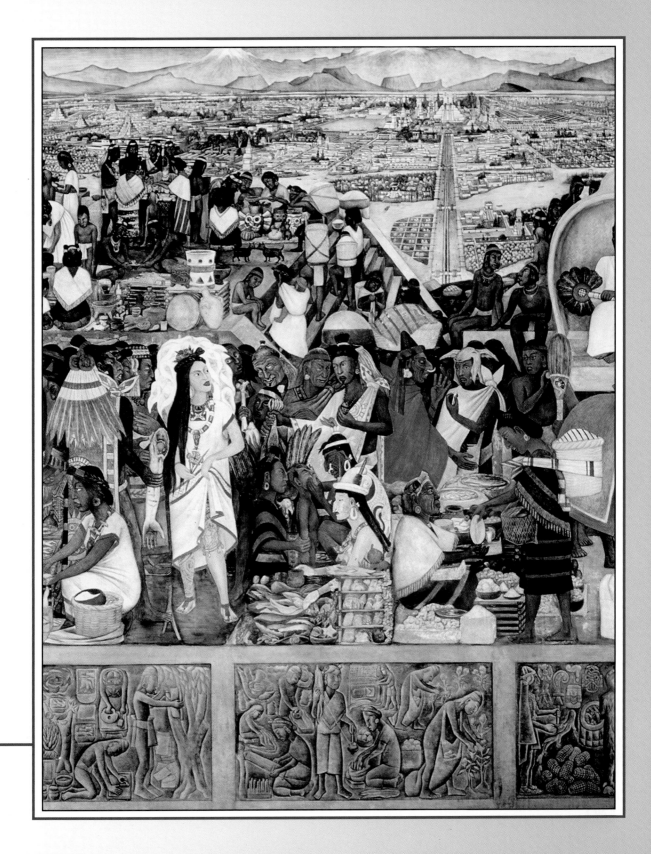

Diego Rivera *(left)*, one of Mexico's most renowned artists, sought to bring art to the people through murals in public places. He used a direct and realist style, combined with social content. Frida Kahlo *(below)*, wife of Diego Rivera, poses in 1931 as she paints a portrait of a San Francisco society woman, which was commissioned by the San Francisco Stock Exchange.

Diego Rivera (1886–1957), one of Murillo's students, is one of Mexico's best-known artists. Beginning his long career painting murals of Mexico, he soon started to create watercolors of scenes of Mexico.

Rivera and other artists revived a style of wall painting called the fresco. Rivera's works became known throughout the world. He was commissioned to paint murals in the United States. Rivera was considered a controversial figure because he often included political and social messages in his works.

Frida Kahlo (1907–1954) is the most widely known female Mexican artist. Kahlo, who married Diego Rivera in 1929, is best known for painting self-portraits. She often incorporated elements of Mexican religious folk art into her paintings.

Arts and Crafts in Mexico

Arts and crafts flood every Mexican market, making it easy for tourists to take home with them a souvenir representative of Mexico's heritage. Available for sale are earthenware pottery, wooden figures, masks, carved onyx, colorful weavings, silver jewelry, and embroidered clothing.

One of the most distinctive art forms in Mexico is Talavera earthenware. Talavera objects, which have been made in Mexico for more than 400 years, take on

Talavera pottery urns, recognized by the strong, intense colors and patterns, are very high-quality earthenware.

many forms—plates, platters, bowls, figures, wall hangings, pitchers, cups, and mugs. Talavera pieces range from inexpensive to very expensive highly detailed pieces. The best earthenware is made in the state of Puebla. Talavera designs are hand painted onto the clay objects before they are fired. Made throughout Mexico, Talavera is exported all over the world.

The state of Oaxaca is a center for Indian-style arts and crafts. The artisans of Oaxaca make a distinctive black pottery that is highly prized by collectors. Weavers make rugs, blankets, and ponchos with traditional Indian designs. Oaxaca also known for its colorfully painted carved wooden animals and figures. In addition to figures, many traditional ceremonial masks are made of wood or pottery and are common in the area. Signed pieces by Oaxacan artists are available and are prized by collectors. Money earned from this work has enabled some artists to improve their living standards.

Bordado, or embroidery, is part of Mexican women's domestic art. Many Mexican women embroider garments and sell their wares at local markets to supplement the family's income.

A Mexican woman in Oaxaca weaves on a backstrap loom. The cochineal process, a traditional method of dying wool, is named for the tiny cochineal insects that are collected, dried, and ground to make colored dye.

Religious folk art is also common in Mexico. The themes include crosses, crucifixes, and religious scenes. Often, the art has a central theme such as Catholic beliefs, which include depictions of Jesus, the Virgin Mary, and various saints. Many times, traditional Indian influences are added to give the religious folk art from Mexico a distinctive flair.

Mexico has a number of communities that cater to artists. San Miguel de Allende in Guanajuato is one such place. Many people from the United States and Europe live in and around San Miguel de Allende. The city is home to art schools, where student may paint in the picturesque Spanish colonial town. For those less artistically inclined, there are opportunities to purchase paintings and other works from local artists.

The town of San Miguel de Allende was named in 1826 after General Ignacio Allende. It was here that the general joined the army of Miguel Hidalgo as chief lieutenant in the fight for Mexico's independence. For this reason, the village is known as the Forge of National Independence.

Mexico is the home of many art galleries and museums. Many showcase local artists. In Mexico City, there are several art museums that house collections featuring well-known artists from around the world. Museums in the city display examples of Indian art from all over Mexico as well as local art.

Carved wooden figures are a popular worldwide export. People in many agriculture villages have switched to crafting folk art in order to fulfill the growing international demand for these wooden figurines.

THE LITERATURE AND MUSIC OF MEXICO

8

Mexican culture continues to have a significant impact in Latin America and the world beyond in literature and music. In addition, many writers from all over the world have spent time in Mexico and have used the country as a setting in their works.

The Codices

The Maya, and to some extent the Aztecs, recorded much of their history in written texts. Some of the writings, which were carved into stone or painted onto pottery, have survived quite well. The Maya also recorded their history on tablets of bark paper. These tablets, called codices, were folded like accordions and painted onto the front and back of bark paper. When the Spanish conquered Mexico, the Catholic Church had all the codices gathered up and burned because it was thought they were the works of the devil. Today, four of these codices are preserved in museums. The texts tells of Mayan history. Sadly, much of the information was lost when the codices were burned by the Spanish.

Pre-Columbian Music

Pre-Columbian civilizations used music during their religious ceremonies. Remains of drums, flutes, rattles, and seashell horns are often found in archaeological sites. The codices that have survived show people playing instruments during ceremonies. In some parts of Mexico, the old musical traditions are still alive; some people still perform on traditional instruments.

A sixteenth-century statue of Xochipelli, Prince of Flowers *(left)*, represents the Aztec god of flowers, maize, love, games, beauty, song, and dance. He is decorated with flowers, which had a symbolic connection to the sun. He sings to himself using rattles that have since been lost. Ancient Aztec clay flutes *(above)* were played to appease the gods. Because music was such an important part of religious ritual, Aztec musicians enjoyed considerable social prestige.

Discovered in 1946 and originally located at the Bonampak Mayan site, this fresco depicts a ceremonial procession of musicians. The Bonampak location contains the best-preserved color murals of any Mayan site.

Colonial Literature

When Cortés and his conquistadors arrived in Mexico in 1519, they recorded some of their adventures. One such work was written in 1568 by Bernal Díaz del Castillo (c. 1498–1568). Castillo's work, *The True History of the Conquest of New Spain*, was not published until 1632. Like Castillo's chronicle, much of the early works dealt with how the Spanish were transforming Mexico into a colony.

One of the greatest writers during the colonial period was Sor (Sister) Juana Inés de la Cruz (1651–1691), a Catholic nun. She wrote plays, satires, philosophical works, and poetry. In 1816, José Joaquín Fernández de Lizardi (1776–1827) published the first Latin American novel, *The Itching Parrot*.

The 1800s

During the 1800s, Mexico and many other Latin American countries were fighting for and gaining independence from Spain and Portugal. In Mexico, many writers wrote patriotic stories and satires as well as poetry that fanned the flames of revolution. During the 1800s, a variety of literary styles began to appear in Latin America. At this time, many

These pages were taken from Bernal Díaz del Castillo's book *The True History of New Spain*, which was written in 1568, many years after the expeditions. It documents his travels with Hernán Cortés. Other reports of the time depict the events in a variety of ways.

Gregorio López y Fuentes's book *El Indio* received Mexico's National Book Prize in 1935. It is often called a "novel of the revolution."

Latin American authors excelled in romanticism, realism, and modernism. Only a few Mexican writers have made significant contributions to the literature of Latin America. However, Latin American literature was important because it exposed Mexicans to many new ideas.

The 1900s

During the 1900s, Latin American writers began to incorporate regional themes and culture into their works. The Mexican Revolution of 1910 inspired the author Mariano Azuela's (1873–1952) novel *The Underdogs*, which explored social conditions in Mexico. In 1935, Gregorio López y Fuentes (1897–1966) wrote *El Indio* (The Indian), which describes the mistreatment of the Indians of Mexico.

The writers of the mid-1900s began to use authentic subject matter and a variety of themes. They experimented with language, exploring the new awareness of cultural identity. This gave rise to one of Mexican's most important poets, Octavio Paz (1914–1998). Much of his work concerns Mexican cultural identity and Mexican history. Octavio Paz also wrote literary criticism and essays on art and politics. He was noted for his insight into people, his elegance with the language, and his broad knowledge. In 1990, Octavio Paz became the first Mexican to receive a Nobel Prize in literature.

The mid-1900s were also a time when Latin American literature received sudden and unprecedented international attention. Carlos Fuentes (1928–) used literary invention in narratives to express cultural heritage. Fuentes's most famous novel, *Our Land*, looked at life in

Octavio Paz was the 1990 Nobel laureate in literature. During this ceremony, President Ernesto Zedillo of Mexico announced the creation of the Octavio Paz Foundation, dedicated to the promotion of cultural research in Mexico.

The rite of the flyers is a tradition in Papantla. Dancers descend, upside down, from the top of a pole as they slowly turn around it. The dancers are part of the festivities for Corpus Christi, a religious holiday that celebrates salvation through the sacrifice of Christ.

modern Mexico. Fuentes also wrote *Where the Air Is Clear* and *The Death of Artemio Cruz*. Both books have been widely translated into other languages and are sold worldwide.

Music and Dance

Dance was an important part of many of the pre-Columbian cultures in Mexico. During religious ceremonies, dances were performed to request luck during hunting, a good harvest, success in marriage, or victory in war. Some of these traditional dances are still performed today.

One of the most spectacular dances is the *voladores de papantla* (flying pole dance). Four men in feathered costumes to represent the four seasons perform to ensure adequate rainfall for crops. They climb to the top of a 100-foot (30-m) pole. A fifth man, atop the pole, plays a flute. The costumed men are secured to the pole by ropes tied to their feet. The four dancers drop off the pole simultaneously. They swing around the pole thirteen times before reaching the ground.

The first mariachi bands date from the eighteenth century in the state of Jalisco. Mariachi bands consist of eight or more musicians who play on holidays or at parties.

These men play the marimba, a type of xylophone introduced by African slaves and adapted by many Latin American countries. A large, concert-size marimba can have up to seventy-eight keys on an irregular rectangular keyboard and weigh about 130 pounds. It takes four musicians to play this instrument.

They make fifty-two rotations. Each represents one week of the year. The voladores is still performed in several parts of Mexico annually.

Corridos (folk songs) first became popular during the colonial period. A kind of oral history, the songs tell stories or legends about the past, including the Mexican Revolution, bandits, famous sheriffs, and struggles between church and state. Corridos, still popular, are performed at fiestas and family gatherings. In the 1900s, Mexican composers incorporated the themes of corridos, as well as ancient music, into their pieces.

Mariachi bands, strolling musical groups that include singers and musicians playing guitars, trumpets, and violins, are very popular. The mariachi tradition began when Spanish priests used music to help teach the Indians about the Catholic religion. By the 1800s, mariachi groups had spread throughout central Mexico. Mariachi music has become a cornerstone of Mexico's musical tradition.

One of Mexico's traditional musical instruments is the marimba. Similar to a xylophone, a marimba is played by tapping a baton on wood or metal strips. Marimbas, which have a distinctly Mexican sound, are popular at fiestas, parties, and weddings. A marimba is sometimes used by two musicians to play a duet. It is often included as part of a band. Typical marimba music is upbeat.

Folk dances are important to every fiesta. The *ballet folklórico* (folk dance) is a rich and colorful tradition in Mexico. Each state and region of Mexico has its own distinctive dances. One of the most familiar is the *jarabe tapatío* (Mexican Hat Dance) in which men and women perform a lively sequence of heel-and-toe tapping and hopping steps. Ballet folklórico is performed in regional costumes. Men wear traditional cowboy clothes with sombreros, and women wear long, flowing colorful skirts.

FAMOUS FOODS AND RECIPES OF MEXICO

9

When most people think of Mexican food, they think of foods like enchiladas, tacos, and burritos. While these are Mexican foods, they do not begin to describe the wide variety of foods available in Mexico. Mexican foods are a mixture of native Indian, Spanish, and French cuisine. All these influences have blended together to make Mexican food extremely tasty.

Mexico is the original home of many foods that are now used around the world. When the Spaniards arrived in Mexico, they took back to Europe a variety of foods that were new to them. Mexico introduced the world to corn, potatoes, tomatoes, vanilla, chocolate, squashes, assorted beans, avocados, peanuts, chilies, guava, coconuts, papaya, and pineapples.

Corn

Corn has been an important part of the diet in Mexico for at least 10,000 years. Today, corn remains important, especially in rural areas. Corn is usually dried after it is harvested from the field. Mexicans prepare the dried corn for eating by softening it in limewater, boiling it, and then grinding it into a fine meal. Corn meal is usually mixed with water to form *masa* (dough). Masa is shaped either by hand or by machine into a flat, thin disk called a tortilla. The tortilla is cooked on a cast-iron or pottery *comal* (griddle). Served with each meal, tortillas are eaten plain or used as an ingredient in many traditional dishes.

Young girls prepare tamales *(left)*. Mexican occasions are celebrated with different types of tamale fillings and forms. Ethnographers have counted forty-two varieties of tamales, including the *zacahuil*, which is three feet long and weighs about 150 pounds. Mexicans' love of baked goods *(see varieties above)* stretches back to the 1820s when the French introduced pastries and bolillos, crusty rolls shaped like a sewing bobbin.

Rice, Beans, Chilies

Rice, beans, and chilies round out the staples of the traditional Mexican diet. Rice is cooked with chicken stock and perhaps peppers, onions, garlic, and tomatoes. Rice is often served as a side dish at lunch and dinner.

Prepared in a variety of ways, beans are often served at every meal, too. Many kinds of beans are grown in Mexico, but the most common are pinto beans and black beans. Beans may be boiled with onions, peppers, garlic, and tomatoes. Prepared this way, beans are called charro beans. Black beans are cooked as a soup and served with onions and cilantro, a leafy herb. Beans may also be boiled, mashed, fried, and refried in lard. Beans are usually eaten using a tortilla as a scoop.

Because most Mexicans like their food spicy, chilies are a big part of Mexican cooking. Chilies are an excellent source of vitamin C as well as a great spicy ingredient. The general rule is that the smaller the chili pepper, the hotter the chili pepper. The most familiar and widely used chili is the jalapeño. Other popular chilies

People shop for bread at a Mexican market. One of the first nonnative foods introduced by the conquistadors was wheat, which was a Spanish staple and religious necessity since it was the only grain recognized by the Catholic Church as being suitable for the Eucharist.

include serranos, chile piquines, and habaneros. Habaneros, the hottest of all the peppers in the world, are mainly used in the Yucatán Peninsula. But not all chilies are hot. One type of mild chili is the poblano pepper, which is often stuffed with shredded meat or cheese, breaded, and fried to make chiles rellenos, a Mexican version of stuffed peppers.

Pan

Pan is the general term for bread in Spanish. Pan can refer to a loaf of bread, a bread roll, or sweet bread (*pan dulce*). A *bolillo* is a short football-shaped roll that is sometimes served with meals or cut in half to make *tortas* (small sandwiches). Pan dulces come in many different sizes and shapes. Some have fillings and others are breadlike with a sweet coating. Breads are usually purchased at a *panadería* or bakery. The typical method for purchasing pan at a panadería is to pick up a tray and a pair of tongs on your way in. You walk around the shop taking what you want off the shelves or out of bins and putting it on your tray. When you've made your selections, you go to the counter and the clerk will tally up what you owe.

Traditional Dishes

Each region of Mexico has its own selection of traditional dishes. Some of the most familiar, found all over Mexico and in the United States, are based on flat tortillas. Tortillas are folded around meat, lettuce, tomato, and cheese to make a taco. Meat or

Pan de Muerto
(Bread of the Dead)

Ingredients

¼ cup milk

¼ cup (4 tablespoons) margarine or butter, cut into 8 pieces

¼ cup plus 2 teaspoons sugar

½ teaspoon salt

1 package active dry yeast

¼ cup very warm water

1 egg

½ teaspoon aniseed

3 cups all-purpose flour, unsifted

¼ teaspoon ground cinnamon

Procedure

Bring milk to a boil and quickly remove from heat. Stir in margarine or butter, ¼ cup sugar, and salt.

In large bowl, mix yeast with warm water until dissolved and let stand 5 minutes. Add the milk mixture.

Separate the yolk and white of the egg. Add the yolk to the yeast mixture, but save the white for later. Add flour to the yeast and egg. Blend well, until dough ball is formed.

Flour a pastry board or work surface very well and place the dough in the center. Knead until smooth. Return to large bowl and cover with dish towel. Let rise in warm place for 90 minutes.

Preheat the oven to 350°F and grease a baking sheet. Knead dough again on floured surface. Divide the dough into four pieces and set one piece aside. Roll the remaining three pieces into "ropes."

On greased baking sheet, pinch three rope ends together and braid. Finish by pinching ends together on opposite side. Divide the remaining dough in half and form two "bones." Cross and lay them atop braided loaf.

Cover bread with dish towel and let rise for 30 minutes. Meanwhile, in a bowl, mix aniseed, cinnamon, and 2 teaspoons sugar. In another bowl, beat egg white lightly.

After 30 minutes, brush top of bread with egg white and sprinkle with sugar mixture, except on crossed bones. Bake at 350°F for 35 minutes. Cool before eating.

These Zapotec women prepare tortillas, a Mexican food staple made of corn or flour. It is estimated that the average Mexican eats more than a pound of corn dough daily, mostly in the form of tortillas.

cheese is rolled up inside a tortilla, then cooked and smothered in chili sauce to make enchiladas. Heaping amounts of meat or beans, onions, lettuce, tomato, and cheese are wrapped in a tortilla, usually flour instead of corn, to make a burrito. Tortillas can be fried flat until they are crispy; topped with refried beans, meat, lettuce, tomato, and cheese; and baked to make *chalupas*. Meat or cheese is rolled into thin tortillas and fried to make *flautas*, which are often served with a dipping sauce. Two flour tortillas are filled with cheese and cooked on a griddle to make quesadillas. Finally, thick tortillas are lightly fried and topped with meat, lettuce, and tomatoes to make *gorditas*.

Masa, the dough used to make tortillas, can also be used to make tamales. Tamales are made of a spicy meat filling surrounded by masa. Tamales are individually wrapped in corn husks or banana leaves, and steamed until done. They are unwrapped just before they are eaten. Popular at lunch and dinner, tamales are sometimes served at breakfast, too.

Salsa, or hot sauce, is standard on every table in Mexico. Salsa is made from tomatoes, onions, garlic, and chili peppers. Salsa made with tomatoes is called *salsa roja*, or red sauce. *Salsa verde*, or green sauce, is made from tomatillos, a green relative of a tomato. Salsa is also made with fruits including papaya or mango. Salsa goes with just about any dish. It is heaped onto eggs, added to tacos, and even eaten plain with chips. American food analysts have reported that salsa now beats ketchup as the most popular condiment in the United States.

Another traditional dish found in many parts of Mexico is mole, a rich sauce that is served over meat, usually chicken or pork. Made of chocolate, cinnamon, spices, nuts, raisins, and chilies, mole can also be used as a sauce poured over enchiladas. Many regions of Mexico have their own versions of mole. Made from a variety of ingredients, moles range from mild to fiery hot, each with its own distinctive flavor.

Afternoon Break

The siesta is a time in the afternoon when people rest or take naps. Siesta usually lasts from after lunch until about 3 or 4 PM. Many stores and businesses close for siesta, which tends to be during the hottest time of the day, the perfect time to relax in the shade. As Mexico becomes more integrated into the global economy, the daily siesta is becoming a lost tradition.

Traditional Drinks

Long before the Spaniards arrived in Mexico, Indians were drinking hot chocolate. To make traditional hot chocolate, cocoa beans are ground up and mixed with sugar and chilies. The paste is dissolved in either hot water or milk. Mexicans also make a drink from masa called *atole*. They dissolve the masa in water and boil the mixture until it is thick. Atole is served either hot or cold.

Another Mexican drink, which is called *horchata*, is boiled and ground-up rice mixed with cinnamon, lime juice, and sugar. Horchata, which is served cold, is a refreshing drink on a hot day.

Coffee is popular in Mexico. Mexicans usually drink their coffee with plenty of milk and sugar. This way of preparing coffee is called *café con leche*. The traditional way to drink coffee is to have three small pitchers brought to the table with a cup. One pitcher holds very strong black coffee, one holds hot milk, and the third holds hot water. Coffee, milk, and water are all added to the cup in the proportion desired, and then sugar is added to taste. Coffee is a popular drink in the morning with breakfast and after supper with dessert.

A number of alcoholic beverages, made from cacti or other plants, are popular in Mexico. Pulque, mescal, and tequila are made by roasting the heart of an agave plant. The juice is squeezed out and allowed to ferment. The fermented juice is distilled. Another alcoholic drink common in Mexico is called *caña* and is made from the fermented juice of sugarcane. Some of the finer tequilas are bottled and sold in Mexico and around the world. Other alcoholic drinks are usually sold locally.

Markets

Shopping for food in Mexico can be a daily event. Fruits and vegetables are bought at open-air markets called *mercados*. Larger towns and cities have permanent mercados, while smaller towns have temporary mercados that open once or twice a

Although Sunday is market day in Mexico, many peasants arrive on Saturday to be close to the shops and booths. Merchandise includes flowers, candy, pine gum, incense, and pottery.

week. Mercados have a number of vendors; shoppers wander through to buy fruits and vegetables from different people.

Tiendas, or small grocery shops, are common throughout Mexico. Tiendas carry basic items, such as rice, beans, some canned foods, and some fruits and vegetables. In rural areas, *conasupos*—stores that sell staples at government-subsidized prices—may be open daily or only one or two days a week. In larger cities, there are *supermercados*, which are just like large grocery stores in the United States and Canada. They sell a wide variety of products from all over the world. Because of NAFTA (the North American Free Trade Agreement), some large chains of U.S.-based grocery stores are opening supermercados in Mexico.

Meal Times

El desayuno, or breakfast, is usually served between 6 AM and 8 AM. A typical breakfast in Mexico includes some type of pan and coffee. Fruit, fruit juice, and tamales may also be served. Brunch, usually a much heartier breakfast, is served between 10 AM and noon. A typical brunch would be eggs, beans, maybe some type of meat, and coffee or juice.

La comida, or lunch, is traditionally the largest meal of the day. Served about 2 or 3 PM, lunch often starts with soup. The main course may be some meat, rice or pasta, beans, and tortillas or pan. At restaurants, a lunchtime special called *comida corrida* is an inexpensive, complete, and hearty meal. The comida corrida at a restaurant changes daily and is usually satisfying.

La cena, or dinner, is usually served in the evening, around 9 or 10 PM. La cena is a light meal that consists of tacos or leftovers from lunch. Sometimes dinner is more like a snack before going to bed.

DAILY LIFE AND CUSTOMS IN MEXICO

10

I n Mexico, the family is the core of the social structure. Families and extended families are close-knit and gather together at holidays and other festive times. It is not uncommon to have several generations from the same family living together in one house. Work is divided up among family members and children. In agricultural areas, the boys work with the men in the fields, and the girls learn cooking and domestic chores from the women.

City Life

About 75 percent of the current population of Mexico lives in urban areas. Mexico City is one of the largest metropolitan areas in the world. Estimates of the population of the Mexico City area range from 17 to 25 million people. It is difficult to count accurately everyone in the city because of the many unofficial settlements. Mexico has nine cities with population figures of more than 1 million. There are approximately sixty other cities in Mexico with populations of more than 200,000 people.

Most cities in Mexico trace their beginnings to Indian villages. Cities in Mexico are built around a *zocalo*, a square or plaza. The official offices of the city governments are located on the plazas, usually tree-covered parks with benches

A Mexican family waits in a bus station *(left)*. Many people travel by bus since it is Mexico's most inexpensive mode of transportation. The Plazuela de los Angeles is located in Guanajuato *(above)*. Guanajuato is one of Mexico's best-preserved cities, known for its intricate network of underground tunnels built by citizens in the 1900s to divert flooding.

Mexico's fourth largest city is Puebla, also known as the City of Tiles. Today this city is famous for the Talavera tiles that decorate churches, homes, and government buildings.

and paved walkways. The plaza serves as a gathering place for families and friends. Street musicians can often be found there. Evenings and Sunday afternoons are reserved for visiting and strolling around the plaza. During festivals, the plaza may be transformed into an amusement park or fair.

The centers of larger cities are filled with high-rise buildings that house offices, hotels, and apartments. However, even in the largest cities, one or more plazas still survive, serving the same function as in smaller cities.

In the older parts of large cities, the buildings are constructed in the Spanish colonial style. Most have small balconies that extend from the windows, and a patio, or courtyard, in the center. In addition to serving as a relaxing oasis, the patio increases ventilation in the building. Usually, the patio has a fountain, flowers, and plants to make it more appealing.

Within the cities are the *barrios*, or neighborhoods. The houses in middle-class barrios usually have walls surrounding them and metal gates for

A rural farmer tills his field with a horse-drawn plow. Much of the farming in Mexico is done without the help of modern equipment.

entrances. The wall provides privacy and security. The houses are usually built of concrete, with one or two stories. Instead of a yard, the grounds may be transformed into a landscape of flowers and ornamental plants. There is often an outside seating area and sometimes a fountain.

By contrast, houses in the lower-class barrios tend to be built of wood, metal, or any available materials. They are often poorly constructed, with only one or two rooms. These barrios usually lack electricity and running water. People here live in very primitive conditions.

Rural Life

About one-quarter of Mexico's population lives in rural areas or in small villages. Mexican farmers live close to their fields. They are usually very poor. Rural areas and small villages, which may be very remote, often lack social services such as health care and schools. Sometimes children are bussed to school. In other instances, the children may go to the nearest town and stay with relatives. Some children may not attend school at all.

Many rural areas have electricity because of government-sponsored rural electrification projects. However, these places may still lack running water. Many people in villages depend on a community well or community-accessed water supply. Because of the difficulties of rural life, many young people go to the cities to live and find work.

The Mayan girls in this photograph wear traditional Mayan *huipiles*, multicolored upper garments.

Clothing

In the urban areas, Mexican men and women wear clothes similar to people in the United States and Canada. In rural areas, the men usually wear blue jeans or work pants, cotton shirts, and boots. The more traditional style of clothes for men is a plain cotton shirt, trousers, and huaraches, or leather sandals. But this style is becoming less common. Men often wear western-style cowboy hats of straw or felt, which are rapidly replacing the more traditional wide-brimmed sombrero. In areas with large numbers of Indians, men still dress in a more traditional style. In cooler areas, it is common to see men wearing ponchos, woven blankets with a slit in the middle for the head. Men also carry sarapes, which are colorful blankets.

In rural areas, Mexican women tend to dress in a traditional style unique to their region or village. Most Mexican women wear simple cotton dresses with embroidered flowers and birds sewn about the neck. In some regions, the embroidery work may be quite elaborate. Some Indians, particularly those in Oaxaca and Chiapas, wear elaborately woven and embroidered *huipiles*, or simple blouses. Huipiles are worn with a skirt made from a length of fabric wrapped around the waist and secured with a belt. Women carry a rebozo, a fringed shawl, to cover their heads. During festivals and fiestas, both men and women wear clothes that are traditional to their region.

For some fiestas, men wear the national costume of Mexico. This is a dark blue *charro* suit made of velvet or doeskin. The suit has a bolero, or short jacket, and tight riding pants with gold or silver buttons. The costume is completed with spurred boots, a long red bow tie, and a sombrero. Women wear the national costume of Mexico, a dress called a *china poblana*. According to legend, the dress is styled after the dress worn by a Chinese princess from the 1600s who was captured by pirates and sold as a

slave in Acapulco to a man from Puebla. Later, she dedicated her life to helping the poor. She combined local Indian style with Chinese style and created the china poblana, which has a long, flowing red and green skirt decorated with beads. It is topped with an embroidered blouse and a brightly colored sash.

The charreada is an important cultural symbol for the country and features equestrian contests, trick and fancy roping, comedians, singers, and musicians.

Family

In Mexico, family is the core of the society. The term "family" refers to the entire extended family, which includes parents, children, grandparents, aunts, uncles, and cousins. Families are very close and gather together often. If one family member is having hard times, the rest of the family helps out and supports that family member. Even in the poorest of conditions, family members will give anything they have to help a relative. Most small business and stores in Mexico are family businesses. Many, if not all, of the employees are related to each other.

Today, about 90 percent of all Mexicans live in a family-supported group. One of the greatest threats to the family group is that many of the young people are leaving home to find work or education in places far away from the family. As the younger generation is becoming more educated and well traveled, they are moving away from home at a greater rate than at any time in Mexico's history.

Compadres and *comadres* are comparable to godfathers and godmothers. The terms literally translate as "cofather" and "comother." These people are close friends of the family who also lend support to and enhance the extended family. Compadres and comadres are considered part of the family.

Growing Up

Childhood experiences in Mexico vary greatly between children in urban areas and those in rural areas. In cities, all but the poorest children live much like urban children in the United States and Canada. They go to school, play with friends, and do chores at home. Poor and rural children have different lives. The boys usually go to school and work in the fields with the men. The girls help with raising the younger children and do household chores and cooking. In both areas, the children usually remain at home until they are married.

In rural areas, girls and boys marry when they are young, usually between the ages of fourteen and sixteen. Some villages have a tradition of arranged marriages with the bride's family providing a dowry. Many of the poor cannot afford the fee for a marriage license so they simply have a church ceremony and live together as husband and wife. The new family often lives in the same village as their parents. In urban areas, it is much more common for marriages to take place when both the bride and groom are in their twenties. It is becoming common for people to wait even later to get married.

La Quinceañera

La Quinceañera is a tradition in Mexico that marks the transition of a girl to a woman. On her fifteenth

In Mexico, young girls celebrate La Quinceañera with a church ceremony followed by a reception. For La Quinceañera, the young girl chooses seven girls and seven boys to be a part of her court.

birthday, a girl celebrates La Quinceañera to acknowledge that she has reached marriageable age. After attending a special mass at church, the girl returns to the church in a full-length dress flanked by her parents, her compadres (godparents), and up to seven chambermaids. After the ceremony, there is either a party or a trip abroad. The party, the most common choice, is often large and has food, a live band, and dancing.

Social Customs

Mexico is a country where being polite is normal. The people are friendly and helpful. This attitude prevails when people say "hello" and "good-bye." Greetings and farewells are times of warmth and affection. Men greet each other with a handshake and an *abrazo*, or hug. Women often hug and kiss each other on the cheeks. These customs are important, and it is considered rude or an insult to ignore them.

Social Conditions

In Mexico there is a wide gulf that separates the highest class from the lowest class when it comes to social conditions. Health care is an area where the difference between the classes is greatest. Those with good jobs and money have access to excellent doctors and hospitals. For the poor, health care is nearly nonexistent. Cities and towns have government-sponsored clinics where basic health care is provided. For the poor living in rural areas, it may be difficult to go to town for health care. Among the poor, malnutrition is common, as is anemia

These men are part of the Zapotec road maintenance crew.

and vitamin deficiency. Diseases such as influenza, malaria, and respiratory illness are common.

Entertainment

The amount of free time available for entertainment depends upon a person's social class. People in higher classes have more free time for entertainment than do people in the poorer classes. Poor people work from dawn until dusk. Fiestas are one form of entertainment enjoyed by everyone. Even the poorest person will take off work for a fiesta to celebrate a special event.

Sports

Mexico has a wide variety of entertainment opportunities. *Fútbol* (soccer) is the most popular sport in Mexico, followed by baseball. Men and boys enjoy playing both sports, and most towns have a soccer field and a baseball diamond or a large field that serves as both. Basketball is also a popular game; even some of the smallest villages have a basketball court. In the smallest villages, the basketball court often doubles as a drying platform for crops such as corn, beans, and coffee.

Bullfighting is still a popular spectator sport. Originally brought to Mexico by the Spanish, bullfights are held during many different festivals. Bullfighting is often considered a sport but it is actually more of an art form. Activities and stages of the bullfight are set and rigorously followed. During a bullfight, the courage of the matador is pitted against the strength of the bull.

Even more popular than bullfighting is the *charrería* (rodeo). Charrerías are held all over Mexico and range from small events to huge extravaganzas. The participants, called *charros*, are considered to be the strongest and bravest men in all of Mexico. The charros show the audience their skills in roping, riding, and branding cattle.

Winter is the season of bullfights, when full-fledged matadors perform at venues such as La Monumental Plaza de Toros. There are three stages of the bullfights. First, the bull is rushed into the arena, where two picadors thrust lances between the bull's shoulders to weaken it. Then they stick long darts into the shoulders to further debilitate the bull. Finally, trumpets announce the arrival of the matador to the arena, and he taunts the bull with his cape until he is able to deliver the *estocada* (killing sword thrust) into the bull's neck.

EDUCATION AND WORK IN MEXICO

11

Schools in Mexico operate from September to June. Students are given time off at Easter and Christmas and during many national holidays. Students are required by law to attend school between the ages of six and fourteen. The school year is divided into two semesters, and students take about eleven courses during the week. The courses are divided into two-hour blocks and the schedule rotates, unlike most schools in the United States and Canada that have one-hour classes at the same time each day. In Mexico, the general term for school is *colegio*. Colegio is a primary or secondary school in Mexico. It should not be confused with American college.

About 85 percent of children attend primary school. Of these, about 80 percent graduate. Of the graduates, roughly 40 percent complete the first level of secondary school or junior high school. Even fewer go on to the second level (high school) and then to higher study. As a result, Mexico has an abundance of poorly educated people in the workforce with few skilled and educated people for mid-level and upper-level jobs.

This portrait of schoolchildren *(left)* was taken in Guanajuato. The Mexican government mandates that children complete school up to the ninth grade. Many children do not continue past this level because parents depend on them to contribute to the family's income. The women *(above)* work in a shrimp factory in Campeche.

In Mexico, 80 percent of the money for education comes from the federal government. Currently there is a push by government officials to expand education to rural towns and eliminate the segregation by social class that prevails in many schools.

Primary Schools

Kindergarten, which is optional, begins when a child is five years old. Kindergarten is designed to prepare students for elementary school.

Primaria, or elementary school, lasts for six years. The approach to education in Mexico is based on schools from Spain and France. This differs from the educational approach in U.S. and Canadian schools. In Mexico, students are taught deductive reasoning. Students learn to go from global concepts to specific goals. Students in Mexico are taught concepts and ideas rather than specific facts. Grades are based on test scores rather than classroom participation. As a result, students have a broad education that emphasizes Mexico, the world, culture, and current affairs.

Secondary Schools

Secondary schools are divided into two levels. *Secundaria*, or junior high, is a three-year school, and *preparatoria*, or high school, is also a three-year school. Secundaria furthers the education received in primaria. Students who graduate from secundaria are more capable of entering the workforce in jobs that require good math or reasoning skills. In secundaria, students often learn job skills such as basic accounting and keyboarding. These students are also prepared to enter preparatoria.

When a preparatoria is run by a university, it offers students the opportunities to acquire the skills and knowledge they need to enter schools of higher education. Preparatoria schools may also be run as technical or vocational schools, where the students learn specific skills for technical or vocational jobs. Students may receive training in construction trades, automobile repair, appliance repair, or office work.

Private Schools

Private schools, which are usually run by the Catholic Church, often have a much more demanding academic curriculum. Students who graduate from private schools can be better prepared to enter upper levels of the workforce or higher education. At private schools, students often learn how to use business machines and computers. Because private schools are not supported by the government, they are expensive. As a result, only the children of wealthy families attend them.

These high school students in Valle de Bravo study in the school's science laboratory. Current government programs have been implemented to improve educational choices for Mexican children.

Higher Education

Universities in Mexico are similar to universities in the United States and Canada. Students take general core curricula courses before entering specialized classes in their chosen field of study. Like students in the United States, students in Mexico work toward earning their bachelor's degrees. They may choose to continue at university to earn a master's degree or doctorate. Many students choose

Shrimp is the country's "pink gold." It has become the main export of the fishing industry. Pelicans surround this boat hoping for scraps.

to study at universities in the United States or Europe to further broaden their education. After completing a university degree, students are prepared for high-level technical and managerial jobs.

Teachers

Teachers are in short supply in Mexico. Salaries are often low, and teachers are required to work for a time in rural schools. Most teachers in primaria have only completed secundaria before attending a teachers' college. In secundaria and higher-level schools, teachers usually have a bachelor's degree. The number of teachers with advanced college degrees, even in a university, is very limited.

Working in Mexico

In 1934, the government passed a law requiring employers to pay workers a minimum wage. Unfortunately, this law is seldom obeyed, and wages are usually below the cost of living. As a result, most families have many members working just to survive. Some

Mexican soldiers march during a military parade on Independence Day. Mexico's armed forces have approximately 225,000 active-duty personnel. Women can serve in the military with the same rights as men, but they are not eligible to serve in combat positions, to be admitted to a service academy, or to be promoted beyond a rank equivalent to major general in the United States.

people hold two or three different jobs. Mexico does not have an unemployment system. If someone is out of work or cannot find a job, he or she must depend on family members for support.

Military Service

All eighteen-year old males must serve in the military in Mexico. Every young man serves either in active service or in the reserves. Mexico has a military force of about 225,000 soldiers. About 75 percent serve in the army, with the rest in the navy and air force. The principal roles of the military in Mexico include national defense, narcotics control, and civil assignments such as road building, search and rescue, and disaster relief. Young men may volunteer for military service at the age of sixteen, with parental consent. Women are urged to join the military; the number of women in the military is increasing.

The Future of Mexico

As Mexico looks ahead, it must deal with many issues. To be more competitive in the global economy, Mexico's system of education must be strengthened to give opportunities to more of its people.

This is a view of the United States–Mexico border, looking towards Nogales, Sonora. Each year, 300 million people cross the United States–Mexico border, which stretches 1,951 miles across the southern edge of America.

MEXICO
AT A GLANCE

HISTORY

Evidence shows that Mexico was inhabited more than 20,000 years ago. The earliest people lived in roaming bands that hunted and fished. About 10,000 years ago, people began to settle into villages and start farming. Their efforts at farming led to many crops—such as potatoes, tomatoes, and corn—that are still used as staples in their diet. As these people settled into villages, they also started to form civilizations.

The first great civilization in Mexico was Olmec. The Olmec civilization flourished between 1200 and 400 BC in present-day Tabasco and Campeche. The Olmecs were responsible for creating many forms of art and pottery, a complex counting system, and a calendar.

In this photo from July 2, 2000, in Juchitepec, Mexico, a woman is leaving a voting station set up at the side of a street. She voted in a close presidential election, which was won by Vicente Fox of the National Action Party (PAN), who was considered an outspoken populist.

After the Olmec civilization declined, three other civilizations sprang up in Mexico. These were the Maya, the Zapotec, and the Teotihucán. These civilizations all flourished around the same time. Their civilizations, which peaked from around AD 250 to AD 900, also had elaborate art, counting systems, and calendars. People built large cities and ceremonial centers. Many of the ruins of these cities have been partially restored and are popular tourist destinations today.

After these civilizations fell, two more civilizations developed in Mexico. The Toltec civilization strengthened and rapidly expanded into areas in the Yucatán that had been inhabited by the Maya. As the Toltec empire grew larger, many problems plagued the civilization and it collapsed. The last great civilization to spring up in central Mexico was that of the Aztecs. They were a highly organized group that rapidly expanded their empire through war. They heavily taxed those who were conquered, and they used captives and slaves in their ceremonies for human sacrifices. When Cortés and the Spanish arrived in Mexico in 1519, they did not successfully conquer the native Indians until they defeated the Aztecs.

The arrival of the Spanish and the defeat of the Aztecs allowed Spain to claim Mexico as a colony. Under Spanish rule, many changes were made in Mexico. Many areas of northern and central Mexico were used for mining. Roads were built to connect mining areas with ports along the coast. Indians were used as slaves to do the work. Spain took many resources from Mexico without giving much in return. The Spanish rule lasted until 1821 when Mexico won its independence.

After winning its independence from Spain, Mexico entered a period of turmoil. As the country struggled to turn itself into a republic, power struggles between political parties caused many problems. During Mexico's struggle to form a government, Mexicans had two revolutions, a war with France, and a war with the United States. Overcoming these obstacles, Mexico finally developed a stable government in 1920.

ECONOMY

The economic system of Mexico is based on a free market economy. In the past, much of its important infrastructure, such as airports, seaports, rail systems, communication systems, and energy and gas production and distribution, belonged to state-owned enterprises. In recent years, many of these industries have been privatized. In 1982, 1,000 state-owned enterprises existed. By 2000, that number had dropped to about 200 state-owned enterprises. The efforts at privatizing and expanding competition continue in areas such as transportation, shipping, telecommunications, and energy production.

As a result of the North American Free Trade Agreement (NAFTA), Mexico has tripled its trade with the United States and Canada. Mexico also has trade agreements with the European Union (EU), Israel, El Salvador, Honduras, and Guatemala. In addition, Mexico is establishing trade agreements with other Latin American countries and Asia to reduce its dependence on NAFTA.

The per capita GDP for Mexico is only $8,500. (Per capita GDP for the U.S. is $36,200.) An estimated 27 percent of the population of Mexico lives below the poverty level. The distribution of wealth in Mexico is uneven. The top 20 percent of the income earners accounts for 55 percent of the income. Mexico has labor force of 38.1 million workers. In urban areas, the unemployment rate is conservatively estimated at 2.5 percent with a much higher underemployment rate.

GOVERNMENT AND POLITICS

Mexico is a federal republic that is divided into 31 states. The federal government is based on the constitution of February 5, 1917. According to the constitution, the government is divided into three branches—executive, legislative, and judicial. The executive branch is made up of the president, who serves as both chief of state and the head of government. The president serves a six-year term that is decided through popular vote. The president appoints, with consent of the Senate, a cabinet whose staff runs the different departments in the government.

The legislative branch is a bicameral, or two house, Congreso de la Union (National Congress). The Cámara de Senadores (Senate) has 128 seats. Half of the seats are filled by senators who are elected through popular vote and who serve a six-year term. The remaining seats are allocated among the political parties based on the popular vote they receive. The Cámara Federal de Diputados (Federal Chamber of Deputies) has 500 seats, with each member serving a three-year term. Three hundred members are elected by popular vote while the remaining 200 seats are allocated among the political parties based on the popular vote they receive.

The judicial branch is made up of the Suprema Corte de Justicia (Supreme Court). The judges are appointed to life terms by the president with the consent of the Senate. A series of federal courts are established throughout the country to hear cases that are based on federal law.

In addition to the federal government, each state has its own government. Each state elects a governor for a onetime six-year term to run its day-to-day affairs. Each state government is further divided into *municipios* (municipalities) that run the day-to-day affairs at a local level.

Mexico has more than a dozen different political parties. The three most popular are the Institutional Revolutionary Party (PRI), the National Action Party (PAN), and the Party of the Democratic Revolution (PRD). The current president of Mexico, Vicente Fox Quesada, is a member of the National Action Party (PAN). Fox is the first president in seventy-one years who is not a member of the PRI. The PRI has been the major political party in Mexico, but in the last several elections, both the PAN and the PRD have been winning more and more elections at the national, state, and local levels.

TIMELINE

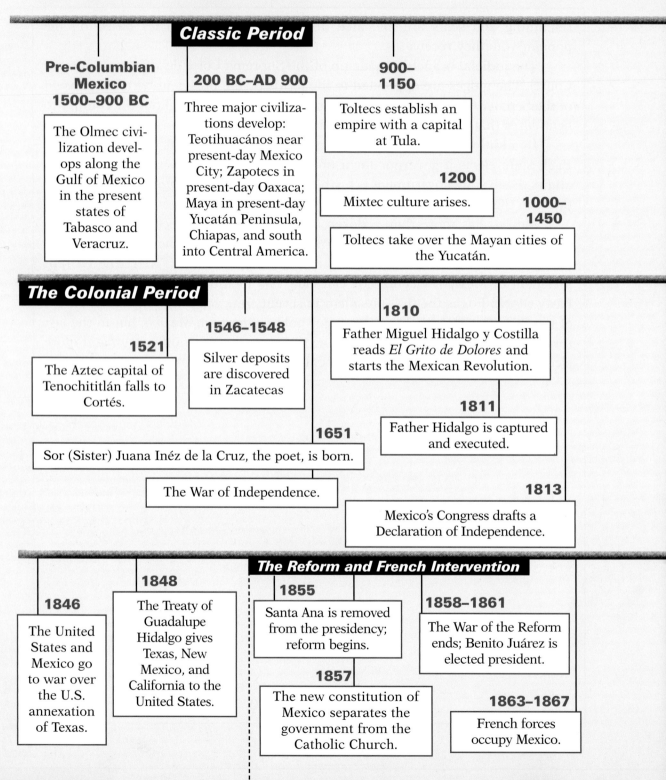

Classic Period

Pre-Columbian Mexico
1500–900 BC

The Olmec civilization develops along the Gulf of Mexico in the present states of Tabasco and Veracruz.

200 BC–AD 900

Three major civilizations develop: Teotihuacános near present-day Mexico City; Zapotecs in present-day Oaxaca; Maya in present-day Yucatán Peninsula, Chiapas, and south into Central America.

900–1150

Toltecs establish an empire with a capital at Tula.

1200

Mixtec culture arises.

1000–1450

Toltecs take over the Mayan cities of the Yucatán.

The Colonial Period

1521

The Aztec capital of Tenochititlán falls to Cortés.

1546–1548

Silver deposits are discovered in Zacatecas

1810

Father Miguel Hidalgo y Costilla reads *El Grito de Dolores* and starts the Mexican Revolution.

1811

Father Hidalgo is captured and executed.

1651

Sor (Sister) Juana Inéz de la Cruz, the poet, is born.

The War of Independence.

1813

Mexico's Congress drafts a Declaration of Independence.

The Reform and French Intervention

1846

The United States and Mexico go to war over the U.S. annexation of Texas.

1848

The Treaty of Guadalupe Hidalgo gives Texas, New Mexico, and California to the United States.

1855

Santa Ana is removed from the presidency; reform begins.

1857

The new constitution of Mexico separates the government from the Catholic Church.

1858–1861

The War of the Reform ends; Benito Juárez is elected president.

1863–1867

French forces occupy Mexico.

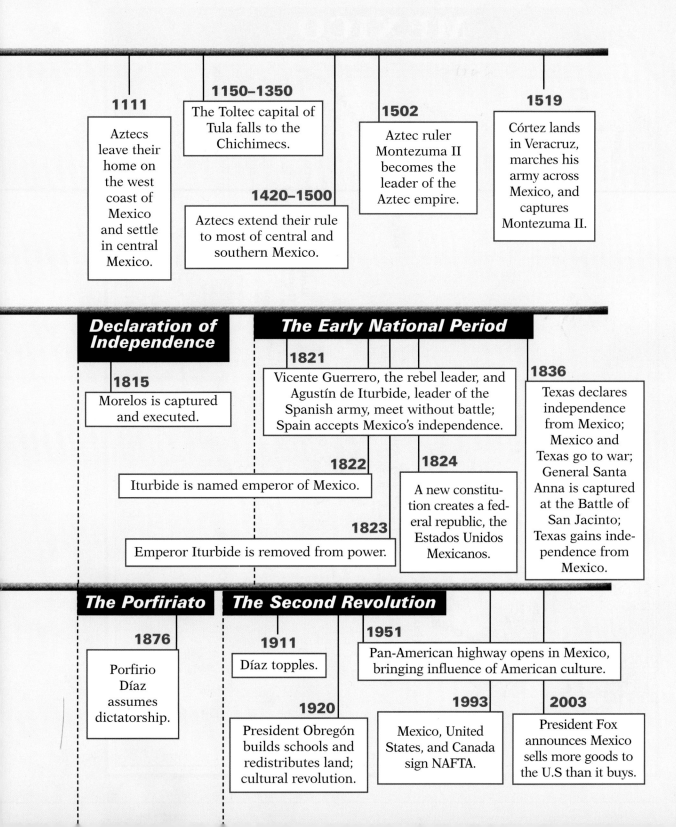

1111

Aztecs leave their home on the west coast of Mexico and settle in central Mexico.

1150–1350

The Toltec capital of Tula falls to the Chichimecs.

1420–1500

Aztecs extend their rule to most of central and southern Mexico.

1502

Aztec ruler Montezuma II becomes the leader of the Aztec empire.

1519

Córtez lands in Veracruz, marches his army across Mexico, and captures Montezuma II.

Declaration of Independence

1815

Morelos is captured and executed.

The Early National Period

1821

Vicente Guerrero, the rebel leader, and Agustín de Iturbide, leader of the Spanish army, meet without battle; Spain accepts Mexico's independence.

1822

Iturbide is named emperor of Mexico.

1823

Emperor Iturbide is removed from power.

1824

A new constitution creates a federal republic, the Estados Unidos Mexicanos.

1836

Texas declares independence from Mexico; Mexico and Texas go to war; General Santa Anna is captured at the Battle of San Jacinto; Texas gains independence from Mexico.

The Porfiriato

1876

Porfirio Díaz assumes dictatorship.

The Second Revolution

1911

Díaz topples.

1920

President Obregón builds schools and redistributes land; cultural revolution.

1951

Pan-American highway opens in Mexico, bringing influence of American culture.

1993

Mexico, United States, and Canada sign NAFTA.

2003

President Fox announces Mexico sells more goods to the U.S than it buys.

MEXICO

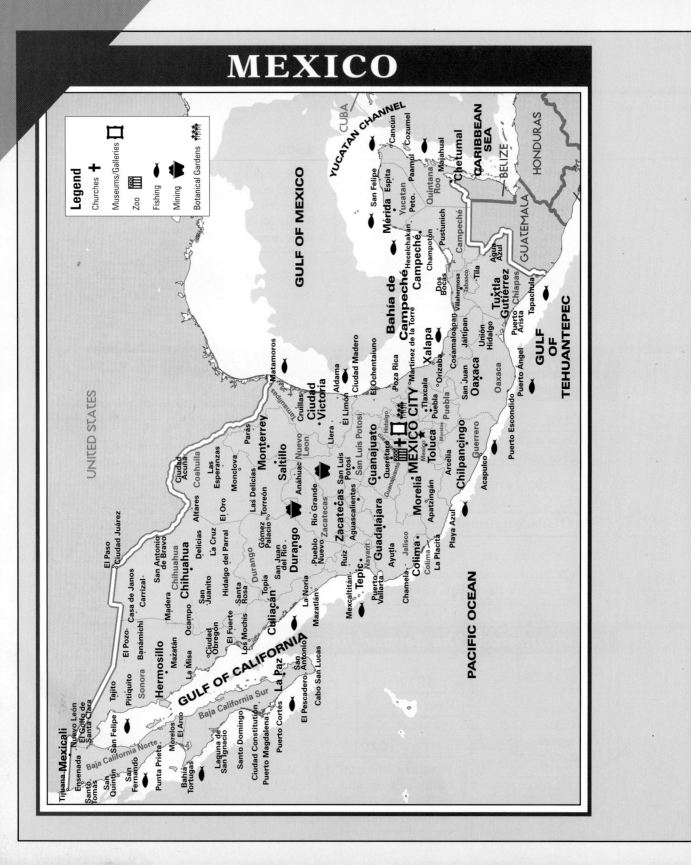

ECONOMIC FACT SHEET

Gross Domestic Product (GDP, 2000): $915 billion
GDP Per Capita (2000): $9,100

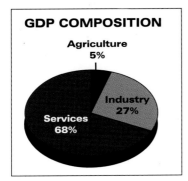

GDP COMPOSITION

- Agriculture 5%
- Industry 27%
- Services 68%

National Budget: $125 billion revenues; $130 billion expenditures
Population Living Below the Poverty Level: 27%
Monetary Unit: Mexican peso
National Workforce (2000): 39.8 million
Unemployment Rate (2000): 2.2%, with higher underemployment rate

Labor Force: Services 56%; industry 24%; agriculture 20%
Major Agricultural Products: Beans, coffee, corn, cotton, fruit, rice, soybeans, tomatoes, wheat; beef, dairy products, poultry; wood products
Major Exports: Manufactured goods, oil and oil products, silver, coffee
Major Imports: Agricultural machinery, aircraft, aircraft parts, electrical equipment, metalworking machines, motor vehicle parts for assembly and repair, steel mill products

Significant Trading Partners:

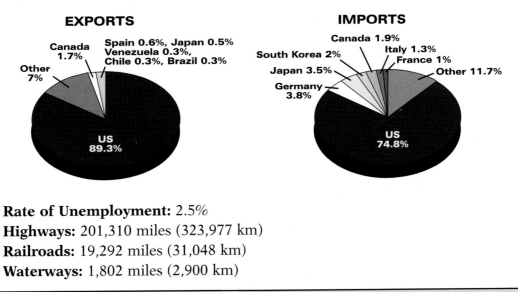

EXPORTS

- Canada 1.7%
- Other 7%
- Spain 0.6%, Japan 0.5%
- Venezuela 0.3%, Chile 0.3%, Brazil 0.3%
- US 89.3%

IMPORTS

- Canada 1.9%
- South Korea 2%
- Japan 3.5%
- Germany 3.8%
- Italy 1.3%
- France 1%
- Other 11.7%
- US 74.8%

Rate of Unemployment: 2.5%
Highways: 201,310 miles (323,977 km)
Railroads: 19,292 miles (31,048 km)
Waterways: 1,802 miles (2,900 km)

POLITICAL FACT SHEET

Official Country Name:
Estados Unidos Mexicanos
(United Mexican States)
Capital: Mexico City
System of Government:
Federal Republic
Federal Structure:
Three branches
executive, legislative, judicial
National Anthem: "Himno
Nacional Mexicano"

*Mexicans, at the cry of battle
lend your swords and bridle;
and let the earth tremble at its center
upon the roar of the cannon.*

*Your forehead shall be girded, oh fatherland,
with olive garlands
by the divine archangel of peace,
For in heaven your eternal destiny
has been written by the hand of God.
But should a foreign enemy
Profane your land with his sole,
Think, beloved fatherland, that heaven
gave you a soldier in each son.*

*War, war without truce against
who would attempt
to blemish the honor of the fatherland!
War, war! The patriotic banners
saturate in waves of blood.
War, war! On the mount, in the vale
The terrifying cannon thunder*

*and the echoes nobly resound
to the cries of union! liberty!*

*Fatherland, before your children
become unarmed
Beneath the yoke their necks in sway,
May your countryside be watered with blood,
On blood their feet trample.
And may your temples, palaces and
towers crumble in horrid crash,
and their ruins exist saying:
The fatherland was made of
one thousand heroes here.*

*Fatherland, fatherland, your children swear
to exhale their breath in your cause,
If the bugle in its belligerent tone
should call upon them to struggle with bravery.
For you the olive garlands!
For them a memory of glory!
For you a laurel of victory!
For them a tomb of honor!*

Voting Age: All Mexican citizens over the age of 18 are eligible to vote.
Voting is universal and compulsory but not enforced.
Number of Registered Voters: 58,789,209 (as of July 2000).
Political Parties: The three most popular parties are the Institutional
Revolutionary Party (PRI), the National Action Party (PAN), and the Party of
the Democratic Revolution (PRD).

CULTURAL FACT SHEET

Population: 101,879,171 (2001)

Age Structure: 0–14 years: 33.32% (male 17,312,220; female 16,635,438)

15–64 years: 62.28% (male 30,888,015; female 32,558,359)

65 years and over: 4.4% (male 1,997,219; female 2,487,920) (2001 est.)

Life Expectancy at Birth: Total population: 71.76 years; male: 68.73 years; female: 74.93 years (2001 est.)

Ethnic Groups: Mestizo (Indian and Spanish) 60%, Indian or predominantly Indian 30%, white 9%, other 1%

Religions: Roman Catholic 89%, Protestant 6%, other 5%

Languages: Spanish, various Mayan, Náhuatl, and other regional indigenous languages

Literacy: Age 15 and over can read and write.
   Total population: 89.6%; male: 91.8%; female: 87.4% (1995 est.)

National Flower: Dahlia

National Bird: Crested caracara

JANUARY
- **1:** Año Nuevo (New Year's Day)
- **6:** Día de los Santos Reyes (King's Day)
- **17:** Feast Day of San Antonio de Abad

FEBRUARY
- **5:** Día de la Constitución
- **24:** Flag Day

MARCH
Carnaval: This five-day celebration is held each year before Catholic Lent.
- **21:** Birthday of Benito Juárez

APRIL
Semana Santa (Holy Week)

MAY
- **1:** Primero de Mayo
- **5:** Cinco de Mayo
- **10:** Mother's Day

JUNE
- **1:** Navy Day

SEPTEMBER
- **16:** Mexican Independence Day

OCTOBER
- **12:** Día de la Raza

NOVEMBER
- **1–2:** Día de los Muertos (Day of the Dead)
- **20:** Mexican Revolution Day

DECEMBER
- **12:** Día de Nuestra Señora de Guadalupe (Day of the Virgin of Guadalupe)
- **December 16–January 6:** Las Posadas
- **25:** Navidad (Christmas Day)

GLOSSARY

atole (ah-TOW-lay) A drink made of cornmeal and water.

cenote (sen-OH-tay) A steep-sided sinkhole that reaches down to water; usually found in the Yucatán Peninsula.

charrería (char-eh-REE-ah) Mexican-style rodeo.

charros (CHA-ros) Mexican cowboy.

codex (KO-dex) A booklet made from bark, folded accordion-style, in which pre-Columbian history was recorded.

conquistadors (kon-KEES-tuh-dorz) Spanish soldiers who conquered Mexico with Cortés.

corridos (kor-EE-dos) Mexican folk songs.

festival (FES-tih-val) A celebration that usually includes music, dancing, and food; they can involve entire cities, states, or regions.

fiesta (fee-ES-tuh) A celebration that usually includes music, dancing, and food; fiestas are celebrations that range in size from small to large gatherings.

hacienda (ah-see-EN-dah) A large estate with a fortified house; hacienda owners usually controlled large areas of land.

henequén (eh-neh-KEN) Fibers from an agave plant that are woven into string or rough fabric.

horchata (or-CHA-ta) A drink made of rice and water.

Indians (in-DEE-inz) People in Mexico who trace their ancestry to a time before the Spanish arrived in 1517.

masa (MAH-sa) A dough made of cornmeal and water used to make foods and drinks.

mestizo (mess-TEE-so) A person with a mixture of Spanish and Indian ancestry.

Náhuatl (nat-oo-AHT-il) A common language spoken by many Indian groups present when the Spanish arrived in Mexico.

pre-Columbian (PREE-co-LUM-bee-an) Before Columbus; before the arrival of the Spanish in Mexico in 1517.

pyramid (PEER-uh-mid) A four-sided temple having stepped sides and a flat top with small chambers on top.

Quetzalcoatl (kwet-suhl-keh-WA-tul) The feathered serpent god, found in many of the Indian cultures of Mexico.

Semana Santa (sem-AH-na SAN-ta) (Holy Week) The week between Palm Sunday and Easter Sunday.

siesta (see-ES-tuh) A period of rest after lunch.

tortilla (tor-TEE-huh) A flat, thin, round disk of cornmeal or flour that is cooked and eaten with all meals.

zócalo (SO-kahl-oh) A central plaza or square in a town or city.

FOR MORE INFORMATION

Consejo de Promoción Turística de México
(Mexican Tourism Board)
1-800-44-MEXICO (1-800-446-3942)
Web site: http://www.visitmexico.com

Embassy of Mexico/Embajada de Mexico
1911 Pennsylvania Avenue NW
Washington, DC 20006
(202) 728-1600
Web site: http://www.embassyofmexico.org/english/

Mexican Government Tourism Office
21 East 63rd Street, Third Floor
New York, NY 10021
(212) 821-0314
1-800-44-MEXICO (1-800-446-3942)
Web site: http://www.mexonline.com/.mxtur.htm
Offices also in Chicago, Houston, Los Angeles,
Miami, and Washington, DC.

Web Sites
Due to the changing nature of Internet links, the
Rosen Publishing Group, Inc., has developed an
online list of Web sites related to the subject of
this book. This site is updated regularly. Please
use this link to access the list:

http://www.rosenlinks.com/pswc/mexi/

FOR FURTHER READING

Beck, Barbara L. *The Ancient Maya*. New York: Franklin Watts, Inc., 1983.

Casagrande, Louis B., and Sylvia A. Johnson. *Focus on Mexico: Modern Life in an Ancient Land*. Minneapolis, MN: The Lerner Publishing Group, 1986.

Dawson, Imogen. *Food and Feasts with the Aztecs* (Food and Feasts). Parsippany, NJ: New Discovery Books, 1995.

Hayes, Joe, and Vicki Trego Hill. *La Llorona (The Weeping Woman): An Hispanic Legend*. El Paso, TX: Cinco Puntos Press, 1987.

Hull, Robert. *The Aztecs*. Austin, TX: Raintree Steck-Vaughn Publishers, 1998.

Hunter, Amy N. *The History of Mexico*. Philadelphia: Mason Crest Publishers, 2003.

Oster, Patrick. *The Mexicans: A Personal Portrait of a People*. New York: William Morrow and Company, 1989.

Reilly, Mary-Jo, and Leslie Jermyn. *Mexico* (Cultures of the World). 2nd ed. New York: Benchmark Books, 2002.

BIBLIOGRAPHY

Barry, Tom, ed. *Mexico: A Country Guide*. Albuquerque, NM: Inter-Hemispheric Education Resource Center, 1992.

Fehrenbach, T. R. *Fire and Blood: A History of Mexico*. New York: Bonanza Books, 1973.

Parkes, Henry Bamford. *A History of Mexico*. Boston: Houghton Mifflin Company, 1960.

Riding, Alan. *Distant Neighbors: A Portrait of a People*. New York: Vintage Books, 1986.

Schlesinger, Arthur M., and Fred L. Israel, eds. *Ancient Civilizations of the Aztecs and the Maya: Chronicles for National Geographic*. Philadelphia, PA: Chelsea House, 1999.

Simon, Joel. *Endangered Mexico: An Environment on the Edge*. San Francisco: Sierra Club Books 1997.

PRIMARY SOURCE IMAGE LIST

Page 18: An Aztec illumination located at the Museo de la Ciudad de Mexico.

Page 19: The statue of the Angel of Independence in Mexico City, Mexico, was designed by Italian artist, Enrique Alciati. Construction on the statue began in 1901.

Page 20: The cave paintings at Cueva Pintada in Baja California were created between 100 BC and AD 1300.

Page 21 (top): Illustration from a Maya codex circa 900 is housed at the British Museum in London, England.

Page 21 (bottom): Olmec statue created between 1200 BC and AD 400.

Page 23: Map of Tenochtitlán designed and drawn by Hernán Cortés circa 1521.

Page 24: A plate from the Mayan city of Campeche is dated between 500 and 800.

Page 26: Atrocities committed by the conquistadors engraved by Theodore de Bry (1528–1598). Located at the Bibliotheque Nationale in Paris, France.

Page 27: Montezuma kneeling before Cortés is portrayed in a 1519 fresco painting by Miguel Gonzalez.

Page 29: The Texas Declaration of Independence, signed March 2, 1836, is located at the Center for American History at the University of Texas at Austin.

Page 30 (top): Treaty of Guadalupe Hidalgo was signed February 2, 1848. It is located at the Library of Congress Manuscript Division in Washington, DC.

Page 30 (bottom): This cartoon by Clifford Berryman, dated 1916, is titled "Carranza and Uncle Sam."

Page 31: This lithograph of Benito Juárez was created between 1857 and 1872.

Page 32: A portrait of Porfirio Diaz dating from 1884.

Page 32: Francisco Madero and his men pose for a photograph taken by Alec Tweedie in the late 1800s.

Page 36: Mural by Diego Rivera (1886–1957).

Page 37: Codex Zouche Nuttall dates between 1350 and 1500 and is located in the British Museum in London, England.

Page 40: Dresden Codex dates from AD 1200 to 1250 and is located in Dresden, Germany.

Page 42: Codex Fejérváry-Mayer is located in the Liverpool Museum, Liverpool, England.

Page 43: The clay statue called the Scribe of Cuilapan was found at the ancient Zapotec site of Quicopecua. It was made between 200 BC and AD 200.

Page 48: A shrine of the Virgin of Guadalupe is located near Punta Chueca, Mexico.

Page 49: A manuscript of *Treasure of the Three Languages*, which was written between 1700 and 1703 by Francisco Ximénez.

Page 51: This Aztec shell mosaic portrays Quetzalcóatl rising from the jaws of Earth (represented by a coyote). It is housed at the National Museum of Anthropology in Mexico City.

Page 62: A wooden statue of the rain god Tlaloc is part of the Philip Goldman Collection, London, England.

Page 63: This Mayan codex circa 900 shows the rain god Chac. It is located in the British Museum, London, England.

Page 64: This limestone inscribed with Mayan hieroglyphs which is located in the National Museum of Anthropology in Mexico City.

Page 66 (top): This illustration from an Aztec codex shows a human sacrifice, dating from the sixteenth century.

Page 66 (bottom): The Aztec calendar, called Stone of the Sun, was carved in 1479. It is located in the National Museum of Anthropology in Mexico City.

Page 68: This copper engraving by Diego de Valadés appeared in his book *Rethorica Christiana* from 1579.

Page 69: Indian slaves are shown laying the foundation for the cathedral in Mexico City. This illustration, dating from 1522, is located in the Biblioteca Nacional in Madrid, Spain.

Page 71: Sculpted from volcanic stone during the Olmec civilization, this statue is thought to portray a warrior.

Page 72: El Castillo, a Mayan temple believed to be linked to the Mayan calendar, is located at ruins of the ancient city of Chichén Itzá, Mexico.

Page 73: Mayan fresco, painted on limestone, depicts Maya raiding a village for victims to sacrifice. It is now located at the National Anthropological Museum in Mexico City.

Page 75: An Aztec eagle bowl, used for storing hearts from sacrificial ceremonies, is located at the National Anthropological Museum in Mexico City.

Page 79: An incomplete mural by Diego Rivera which is located in the National Palace in Mexico City.

Page 84: A sixteenth century Aztec statue of Xochipelli, Prince of Flowers, is located at the National Museum of Anthropology in Mexico City.

Page 86 (bottom): Pages from Bernal Díaz del Castillo's book *The True History of New Spain* written in 1568.

INDEX

About the Author

Allan B. Cobb is a science writer and archaeologist living in Hawaii. His writing includes books, radio scripts, scientific articles, and educational materials covering aspects of science and archaeology. He enjoys traveling, camping, hiking, boating, and caving.

Designer: Geri Fletcher; **Cover Designer:** Tahara Hasan; **Editor:** Jill Jarnow;
Photo Researcher: Gillian Harper; **Photo Research Assistant:** Fernanda Rocha